CHEFS of ALOHA

Favorite Recipes from
the Top Chefs of Hawai'i

Acknowledgments:

"Hot California Rolls with Kona Lobster Mousse...but with No Rice!" (pp. 28-29) reprinted with permission from *Alan Wong's New Wave Luau* by Alan Wong. Copyright ©1999 by Alan Wong, Ten Speed Press, Berkeley, CA, www.tenspeed.com.

"'Poky Pines': Crispy Ahi Poke with Avocado, Wasabi Soy Sauce, Togarashi Aioli, and Tarragon-Tobiko Vinaigrette" (pp. 50-51) reprinted with permission from *Alan Wong's New Wave Luau* by Alan Wong. Copyright ©1999 by Alan Wong, Ten Speed Press, Berkeley, CA, www.tenspeed.com.

"Thai Hot and Sour Miso Soup with Shrimp Dumplings" (pp. 64-65) reprinted with permission from *Roy's Feasts from Hawaii* by Roy Yamaguchi and John Harrison. Copyright ©1995 by Roy Yamaguchi, Ten Speed Press, Berkeley, CA, www.tenspeed.com.

Photo of "Thai Hot and Sour Miso Soup with Shrimp Dumplings" (p. 64) reprinted with permission from Lois Ellen Frank. Copyright ©1995 by Lois Ellen Frank. Reprinted from *Roy's Feasts from Hawaii* by Roy Yamaguchi and John Harrison, Ten Speed Press, Berkeley, CA, www.tenspeed.com.

"Hawaiian Vintage Chocolate Crunch Bars" (pp. 140-141) reprinted with permission from *Alan Wong's New Wave Luau* by Alan Wong. Copyright ©1999 by Alan Wong, Ten Speed Press, Berkeley, CA, www.tenspeed.com.

Published and distributed by

ISLAND HERITAGE
PUBLISHING
94-411 KŌʻAKI STREET, WAIPAHU, HAWAIʻI 96797
ORDERS: (800) 468-2800
INFORMATION: (808) 564-8800
FAX: (808) 564-8877
islandheritage.com

ISBN# : 0-89610-398-6

Second Edition, First Printing - 2003

CONTENTS

Cover: Macadamia Nut-Crusted Mahimahi with Chili Coconut Butter Sauce, Sesame Potato Cakes and Sautéed Spinach
Title page: Hot California Rolls with Kona Lobster Mousse … But with No Rice!

People in Hawai'i love to eat. From weddings and birthdays to graduations and anniversaries, food is a major part of virtually every occasion. Menus reflect the ethnic diversity of the Islands' population; tables piled high with *maki* sushi, Chinese noodles, teriyaki chicken wings, potato/macaroni salad and pipikaula are standard at many gatherings.

For generations, immigrants from Europe, the U.S. mainland, Puerto Rico, China, Japan, the Portuguese Azores and Madeira, Korea and the Philippines shared *bento* (box lunches), and eventually marriage beds, on sugar and pineapple plantations. The "chop suey" cuisine that resulted held only a passing resemblance to what they'd left back in their home countries.

Unable to find just the right ingredients and sauces in Hawai'i, they improvised or created their own recipes based on memory. The bounty they shared from their backyard gardens was used in many different ways; for example, half-ripened mangoes became chutney for curries laced with coconut milk, or "mango seed," a substitute for a confection from China, which is marinated in Hawaiian salt, lemon peel, *li hing mui*, five spices, brown sugar, lemon juice, cloves and a dash of whiskey.

Out of this cosmopolitan culture, the plate lunch was born. Two things were essential for every plate lunch—two scoops of steamed white rice and another scoop of macaroni salad (slightly overcooked with lots of mayonnaise). To that was added any combination of meats that was desired, from hot dogs to shoyu chicken to thin slices of grilled teriyaki beef.

This simple but satisfying meal was available at small neighborhood food stands and lunch wagons everywhere in the Islands. In addition, inexpensive canned goods like Spam, vienna sausage and corned beef were basics on pantry shelves. It was a world of food that belonged almost solely to the local culture.

Meanwhile, until the late 1980s, Island hotels were serving visitors their version of "Hawaiian food"—grilled mahimahi, fresh pineapple spears and white coconut cake. Not that this was all that bad. After all, tourists weren't vacationing here for the food. Hawai'i's sun, surf and laid-back lifestyle had a much more powerful appeal.

Then a little over a decade ago, change came on the heels of a revolution in California, where celebrated chefs began favoring fresh, locally grown products. Young chefs arriving to work in top Hawai'i hotels and restaurants also wanted to cook with more regional ingredients. Like their counterparts on the West Coast a few years earlier, they were surprised to discover that they couldn't buy the simplest fresh Island produce or fish. Everything was shipped in at great expense from the mainland. The ubiquitous mahimahi filet was most likely frozen and from Southeast Asia.

The chefs started talking to each other and comparing notes. They attended fish auctions and began experimenting with varieties never before prepared in restaurants such as kajiki, opah and shutome. They persuaded farmers to try growing baby greens, tomatoes, onions and other vegetables. Hotel executives agreed to set aside small plots of land on property so their chefs could plant herb gardens.

In their kitchens, the chefs began paying attention to the food their local help prepared for themselves after hours. It was a revelation. Before long, these Island chefs were turning the heads of guests and food editors at top magazines. Thus, Hawai'i Regional Cuisine was born.

Hawai'i is now witnessing yet another exciting wave of innovation in the kitchen. Most of the first pioneering chefs hailed from elsewhere, and the dishes they created were a variation of the classic cuisine they were trained to do. The Islands' newest innovators are primarily locally born and schooled, and instead of looking to classic cuisine for inspiration, they are frequenting their mothers' kitchens and plate lunch diners. They are paying attention to their own ethnic backgrounds, and in the process are coming up with imaginative twists on the humble *musubi* and poke.

Simple chili pepper water has moved onto the tables at award-winning restaurants like Alan Wong's, poi lavosh can be found on the shelves of major supermarkets, and kālua pig is a popular topping for freshly baked pizza. Both kamaʻāina and visitors are embarking on exhilarating new dining adventures led by the Chefs of Aloha.

Where this new breed of culinary wizards will go next is anyone's guess. What we do know is that Hawaiʻi's melting pot continues to sizzle, providing rich cultural diversity and endless food for thought. Immigrants keep coming to Hawaiian shores—this time from Vietnam, Thailand, Mexico and the South Pacific. No doubt, they too will have something tantalizing to add to the dynamic mix.

When using this book, be fearless. If you don't have an ingredient, improvise. If a recipe seems complex and daunting, use just part of it. Make the sauce or marinade, and forget about the rest. You can't make a mistake. Simply taste as you go along.

Hawaiʻi's contemporary cuisine is inclusive. Everyone is welcome to discover, enjoy and contribute. The journey to more delicious and ever more exotic flavors has only begun. Let's all join in and celebrate it!

APPETIZER

Kālua Duckling Pot Stickers

'AHI CAKES

With Roasted Sweet Corn Relish

SERVES 4

1 lb. fresh 'ahi, finely chopped	2 tsp. sambal olek	Salt and pepper to taste
½ cup diced onion	2 tsp. lime juice	Roasted Sweet Corn Relish
¼ cup finely sliced green onion	2 Tbsp. Worcestershire sauce	(see recipe below)
2 Tbsp. chopped cilantro		

In a bowl combine all ingredients, except Roasted Sweet Corn Relish; mix well. Use a small ice cream scoop to portion out the mix, directly into a hot sauté pan with some oil. Cook for about one minute on each side. Serve hot with Sweet Corn Relish.

ROASTED SWEET CORN RELISH

2 pcs. sweet corn on the cob, roasted	¼ cup diced green bell pepper	½ cup olive oil
1 cup diced papaya	¼ cup diced sweet onion	2 Tbsp. cilantro
¼ cup diced red bell pepper	¼ cup balsamic vinegar	Salt and pepper to taste

Cut corn off the cob into a bowl and mix in all the remaining ingredients. Season to taste with salt and pepper.

'AHI TARTARE AND WASABI TOBIKO

SERVES 4

1   lb. 'ahi, diced into ¼" pieces
Dressing (see recipe below)
6   slices white bread, toasted
6   tsp. wasabi tobiko
6   slices taro, thinly sliced and fried
Ponzu Sauce (see recipe below)

Tony Novak-Clifford

In a bowl combine 'ahi and dressing; toss lightly to mix ⚬ Cut the toast with a 3" cake cutter and leave the piece of bread inside ⚬ Using the cutter as a mold, fill the mold with the 'ahi mixture up to ¼" from the top and finish with a teaspoon of wasabi tobiko ⚬ Remove the 'ahi tartare from the mold and place on a plate ⚬ Repeat the procedure for each serving. Decorate with the taro chips ⚬ Surround with Ponzu Sauce.

DRESSING

3 Tbsp. sherry vinegar	1 Tbsp. minced shallot	1 tsp. ground coriander
2 Tbsp. finely chopped chives	½ cup extra virgin olive oil	Salt and pepper to taste

In a mixing bowl combine all ingredients and blend well.

PONZU SAUCE

YIELDS ABOUT 1 QUART

½ cup mirin	1 tsp. lemon juice	1 Tbsp. cornstarch, dissolved in
1 Tbsp. soy sauce	Pinch of crushed red chili pepper	two tablespoons of water

In a saucepan combine mirin, soy sauce, lemon juice and chili ⚬ Bring to a boil, then add cornstarch mixture and simmer for 5 minutes ⚬ Reserve at room temperature.

'AHI TEMPURA

With Wasabi Ginger Infusion, Asian Greens and Crisp Wonton

SERVES 6

2 sheets nori	4 cups panko bread crumbs	2 Tbsp. shiracha chili sauce
8 oz. fresh 'ahi (tuna) loin	1 quart canola oil for deep-frying	1 tsp. black sesame seeds
Salt and pepper to taste	Wasabi Ginger Infusion (see recipe	½ cup wontons, julienne, fried
1 cup flour for dusting	on next page)	crisp
3 cups Tempura Batter	2 cups Asian greens (or spicy	
(see recipe below)	mix greens)	

Place nori sheets on a dry surface ▰ Season 'ahi loin with salt and pepper ▰ Place 'ahi at one end of nori and roll up ▰ Seal by moistening edge with water ▰ Dust nori rolls with flour, dip into tempura batter, then panko ▰ Reserve for frying ▰ In a deep fryer or skillet heat oil to 350°F ▰ Using tongs, place 'ahi roll in hot oil for about three minutes or until golden brown ▰ Place on absorbent paper and let drain ▰ With a sharp knife, cut into half-inch slices ▰ Place 1½ ounces of Wasabi Ginger Infusion in center of a warm plate ▰ Top with Asian greens ▰ Add three slices of 'ahi tempura around the greens, then drizzle with shiracha ▰ Sprinkle with black sesame seeds and crispy wonton strips.

TEMPURA BATTER

½ cup flour	¼ tsp. salt
1 cup ice water	1 egg
½ cup cornstarch	

In a medium bowl combine all ingredients and mix well, making sure the batter is not too thick ▰ If too thick, then add more ice water.

WASABI GINGER INFUSION

1	tsp. canola oil	2	cloves garlic, diced	⅓	cup soy sauce
2	shallots, diced	2	Tbsp. wasabi paste	½	cup heavy cream
1	Tbsp. chopped lemongrass	½	cup white wine	1	cup unsalted butter
3	Tbsp. chopped fresh ginger	½	cup rice wine vinegar	1	Tbsp. chopped fresh chives

In a medium saucepan heat canola oil and sauté shallots, lemongrass and ginger until tender ♨ Add garlic and cook a few minutes ♨ Stir in wasabi paste, white wine, rice wine vinegar and soy sauce ♨ Reduce mixture to ¾ cup, then add heavy cream ♨ Reduce to 1 cup, then remove from heat and whisk in butter in small amounts ♨ Strain through a fine strainer ♨ Add chopped chives and reserve for service.

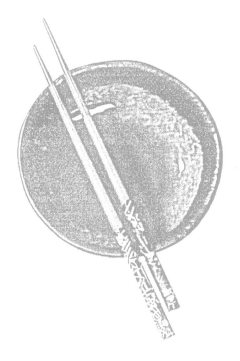

ASIAN ROCK SHRIMP

With Ginger Lime Chili Butter and Cilantro Pesto

Steve Brinkman

SERVES 5

13 oz. raw rock shrimp or other shrimp	Dash of black pepper
½ tsp. lemon juice	Dash of Tabasco sauce
1 egg	Chinese cake noodles or fresh angel hair pasta
2 cups panko flakes	Oil for deep-frying
1 tsp. Dijon mustard	Ginger Lime Chili Butter (see recipe below)
1 Tbsp. chopped green onions	
3 oz. bamboo shoots, chopped	Cilantro Pesto (see recipe below)
1½ oz. mayonnaise	Sprinkle of shichimi

In a bowl combine rock shrimp, lemon juice, egg, panko flakes, Dijon mustard, green onions, bamboo shoots, mayonnaise, black pepper and Tabasco sauce; blend well ❧ Divide into ten equal portions and form cakes ❧ Coat individual cakes with noodles ❧ Fry until golden brown ❧ Coat each appetizer-sized plate with the Ginger Lime Chili Butter ❧ Dot with Cilantro Pesto ❧ Sprinkle with shichimi ❧ *(Note: Shichimi is Japanese 7-spice pepper and is available at Asian grocery stores or in the Asian food section of the supermarket.)* ❧ Top with two shrimp cakes ❧ Enjoy!

GINGER LIME CHILI BUTTER

1 tsp. minced shallots	Juice of one lime	¼ lb. unsalted butter
¼ cup white wine	1 tsp. roux	¼ cup sweet Thai chili paste
1 tsp. chopped fresh ginger	3 oz. heavy cream	

Sauté shallots ❧ Add wine, ginger and lime juice ❧ Reduce by half ❧ Add roux, then add heavy cream ❧ Reduce by half ❧ Whip in butter ❧ Strain, then stir in Thai chili paste and mix well.

CILANTRO PESTO

1 oz. macadamia nuts, chopped	½ cup virgin olive oil	Dash of salt
1 Tbsp. lime juice	1 tsp. chopped garlic	Dash of white pepper
1 oz. fresh cilantro, chopped	1 tsp. chopped ginger	

In a food processor or blender blend all ingredients together at high speed until smooth.

BLACKENED FRESH 'AHI SUMMER ROLLS

With Soy Ginger Sesame Sauce

SERVES 4

4 strips of fresh 'ahi (pink tuna) about 10 inches long (3 oz. each)

Cajun spice to taste

4 pieces Thai rice paper (12 inch diameter)

1 oz. enoki mushrooms

1 oz. radish sprouts

1 oz. shredded carrots

1 oz. shredded beets

1 oz. shredded green mango

16 mint leaves

4 oz. baby lettuce

Soy Ginger Sesame Sauce (see recipe below)

Jon Fujiwara

Sprinkle fish evenly with Cajun spice Heat a nonstick pan and quickly sear the fish for about 10 seconds; set aside Soften each piece of Thai rice paper by spraying it with water or covering it with a damp cloth It will take about 30 seconds to soften Lay them on a flat surface Divide all the ingredients to be wrapped into four portions Layer the ingredients in the following order: enoki mushrooms, radish sprouts, shredded carrots, shredded beets, shredded green mango, 4 mint leaves, 1 piece 'ahi and baby lettuce Roll the rice paper from one end to the other, then roll the rice paper over to form a tube with all the ingredients wrapped inside Repeat for each piece of rice paper and then cut each roll into bite-sized pieces Serve with Soy Ginger Sesame Sauce.

SOY GINGER SESAME SAUCE

¼ cup low sodium soy sauce

¼ cup cooking mirin (Japanese sweet rice wine)

½ cup water

1 oz. sliced fresh ginger

1 oz. sliced onions

1 oz. sliced celery

1 oz. sliced carrot

Dash of sesame oil

2 Tbsp. unsalted butter

In a saucepan combine all the ingredients, except butter Bring to a boil, then reduce heat and simmer for about 20 to 30 minutes Just before serving, strain out the vegetables Slowly whip butter into the remaining sauce Turn off the heat.

Chef's Suggestion: Butter should be at room temperature. When adding butter to the sauce whip continuously until the butter is incorporated into the sauce. Turn off the heat right away.

EDWIN GOTO | THE MANELE BAY HOTEL

CEVICHE OF JAPANESE HAMACHI

With Coconut Milk and Twice-Cooked Green Plantains

SERVES 4

2   Tbsp. coconut milk
1   Tbsp. finely diced red or green
      jalapeno
2   Tbsp. chopped cilantro

2   Tbsp. finely diced Maui onions
Juice of ½ lime
½   lb. Japanese hamachi

Kosher salt to taste
Freshly ground black pepper to taste
Twice-Cooked Green Plantains
  (see recipe below)

In a medium-sized bowl combine coconut milk, jalapenos, cilantro, Maui onions and lime juice ❧ Mix well to remove any lumps from coconut milk ❧ Gently fold hamachi into the dressing and season to taste with salt and black pepper ❧ Allow this mixture to rest for no more than 15 minutes ❧ Top cooked plantains with hamachi and serve immediately.

TWICE-COOKED GREEN PLANTAINS

1   qt. canola oil for frying
3   green plantains

Kosher salt to taste
Freshly ground black pepper to taste

Place a large frying pan with a thick bottom over medium-high heat ❧ Check the oil temperature with a thermometer; it should register 350°F ❧ With a sharp paring knife, cut lengthwise incisions through the skin of the plantain ❧ Peel off the skin and cut plantains in 1" sections ❧ Gently place plantains into hot oil and fry until tender, about two minutes on each side ❧ Remove plantains with a slotted spoon onto absorbent paper towels ❧ Using a small pot with a flat bottom, firmly press plantains to flatten them out to ¼ inch.

Return plantains to hot oil and fry for about 3 minutes on each side ❧ Remove to paper towels and season with salt and pepper.

CHILLED GAZPACHO

With Spicy 'Ahi Tartare

SERVES 6

1 lb. tomatoes, chopped	2 oz. lemon juice	Salt and pepper to taste
4 oz. onion, diced	1 oz. olive oil	Spicy 'Ahi Tartare (see recipe below)
4 oz. red bell pepper, diced	1 Tbsp. lime juice	Cilantro sprigs and tobiko caviar
6 oz. cucumber, peeled, seeded and diced	1 quart tomato juice	for garnish

In a food processor or blender combine tomatoes, onion, red bell pepper, cucumber, lemon juice, olive oil and lime juice; blend well. Add tomato juice and season to taste with salt and pepper. Place a scoop of Spicy 'Ahi Tartare in a shallow soup bowl. Ladle the soup around the tartare. Garnish with cilantro sprigs and tobiko caviar.

SPICY 'AHI TARTARE

½ lb. sashimi-grade 'ahi	2 Tbsp. chopped scallions	2 tsp. sambal olek
2 Tbsp. extra virgin olive oil	1 Tbsp. chopped cilantro	2 tsp. tobiko caviar

Chop 'ahi into fine dice. In a small bowl combine scallions, cilantro, sambal olek and tobiko caviar; blend well. Add olive oil and 'ahi and toss lightly to mix.

MARK ELLMAN | MAUI TACOS

CLAMS GARLIC BLACK BEAN SAUCE

SERVES 2

1 Tbsp. olive oil or sesame oil	1 tsp. fermented black bean, rinsed and chopped	2 oz. white wine
1 tsp. chopped garlic		2 oz. unsalted butter
1 tsp. chopped ginger	Hot chili to taste	¼ cup julienne green onions
1 tsp. chopped Maui onion	1 lb. clams, well rinsed	

Heat a wok to medium-high heat; add oil and sauté garlic, ginger, onion and black beans ✧ Add chili ✧ Add clams, white wine and butter ✧ Cover for one to two minutes until clams open ✧ Stir in green onions.

Steven Minkowski

17

CRAB AND MANGO SALAD HAND ROLL

With Cilantro Thai Vinaigrette

MAKES 4 ROLLS

4½ sheets colored mamenori (soybean wrap)
4 oz. fresh Kula greens (mesclun, exotic, mower)

8 oz. snow crabmeat
3 oz. dry roasted peanuts
4 oz. fresh mango, diced

1 oz. cooked rice
Cilantro Thai Vinaigrette (see recipe below)

Place the mamenori on a work surface with the short end closest to you. In the closest third, lay the greens, crabmeat, peanuts and mango. Dot the top with rice. Using a sushi mat, roll lightly but firmly. Cut in half, place upright, and spoon vinaigrette around the roll.

CILANTRO THAI VINAIGRETTE

2 oz. sake
½ oz. sugar
6 oz. rice vinegar
1 oz. fish sauce

¾ tsp. chopped garlic
1 tsp. sambal olek (garlic chili paste)

2 oz. cucumber, thinly sliced
½ oz. cilantro, coarsely chopped

Burn alcohol off sake, add sugar, and cook until dissolved. In a food processor or blender combine sake mixture, rice vinegar, fish sauce, garlic and sambal olek; blend well. Stir in cucumbers and cilantro by hand.

MARK ELLMAN | MAUI TACOS

FOIE GRAS

With Hayden Mango and Ginger

SERVES 1

3	oz. foie gras steak, scored	1	oz. plum wine		Fresh chopped chervil
¼	mango, peeled and fanned out	4	oz. duck stock		Salt and pepper to taste
2	tsp. chopped shallots	1	oz. pinot noir		Garnish: Moloka'i sea salt and
1	tsp. minced ginger	1	tsp. butter		fresh Hayden mango

Heat a sauté pan on high and sear foie gras for two minutes, one minute on each side. Remove and keep warm. Meanwhile, brown mango under broiler until golden brown. Remove most of the fat from the pan and add shallots and ginger, then deglaze with plum wine. Add duck stock; reduce by half. Add pinot noir and reduce until desired consistency. Swirl in butter and chervil. Correct seasoning with salt and pepper. Sauce plate and top with foie gras. Sprinkle with a little Moloka'i sea salt on top and garnish with mango.

FRESH SALMON TARTARE

With Lemon Dill Cream Sauce

SERVES 8

2	Tbsp. chopped fresh dill	1	salmon filet (about 3 lbs.)		Salt and pepper to taste
6	Tbsp. sugar	4	Tbsp. sour cream		Garnish: lemon slices, fresh
3	Tbsp. salt	1	Tbsp. Dijon mustard		dill, cucumber fans,
1	Tbsp. grated lemon zest	2	Tbsp. lemon juice		black and red caviar

Combine 1¾ tablespoons dill, sugar, salt and lemon zest in a mixing bowl; set aside ❧ In a flat pan coat salmon with the seasoning evenly on both sides to cure the fish, then let sit overnight or at least 4 hours ❧ Completely remove seasoning coat from salmon and chop into little pieces; set aside ❧ In another mixing bowl prepare the sauce by combining sour cream, Dijon mustard, lemon juice and the remaining ¼ table-spoon dill, salt and pepper ❧ Mix ¾ of the sauce with the chopped salmon and form the fish into any shape you prefer ❧ Garnish the salmon tartare with a slice of lemon, fresh dill, cucumber fan, and black and red caviar ❧ Use remaining lemon dill sauce as a condiment ❧ A piece of toast or crisp cracker is a perfect complement to this dish.

Jon Fujiwara

GINGERED CRABMEAT AND TOBIKO CAVIAR NAPOLEON

SERVES 2

6 oz. Dungeness crabmeat
2 Tbsp. tobiko caviar
⅛ cup diced green onions
2 Tbsp. mayonnaise

1 tsp. finely grated ginger
Salt and pepper to taste
6 wonton pi, cut into eighths

Oil for shallow frying
2 green onions for garnish
2 tsp. black sesame seeds

In a stainless steel bowl combine crabmeat, caviar, diced green onions, mayonnaise and ginger. Season to taste with salt and pepper. Let rest for about ½ hour for the flavors to develop. Fry wonton pi in oil preheated to 350°F until golden brown. Be sure to turn wonton pi over, so both sides are nice and brown. Spoon crab mixture onto the center of one wonton pi. Place a wonton pi on top and add more crab mixture. Top with another piece of wonton pi and garnish with green onions and black sesame seeds.

GRILLED TEPPANYAKI AND OYSTERS

With Rainbow of Caviar

SERVES 2

6	fresh oysters
1	cup fresh spinach leaves, stems removed
2	oz. smoked bacon, diced
2	Tbsp. diced onion
1	Tbsp. fresh minced garlic
2	oz. béchamel sauce
	Salt and pepper to taste
	Juice of lemon
2	Tbsp. wasabi tobiko
2	Tbsp. chili pepper tobiko
3	oz. Hawaiian salt
1	drop blue food coloring
2	sprigs parsley
3	green onions, thinly sliced into threads

Shuck oysters and rinse in fresh cold water, reserving half of the shells. Set aside in refrigerator until ready to use. Blanch spinach in boiling hot, salted water for 15 seconds and cool immediately in a strainer. Squeeze excess water from leaves and coarsely chop. Heat skillet and sauté smoked bacon until 75 percent cooked, then add onion and sauté until transparent. Stir in garlic. Fold in béchamel sauce and adjust seasoning. Season oysters with salt and pepper; grill. Add lemon Juice. Place oyster shells on grill to heat and top with a heaping tablespoon of spinach mixture. Top with cooked oyster and finish dish with two flavors of tobiko. Place oysters on rock salt colored with blue food coloring. Garnish with parsley and green onion threads and serve immediately.

HANA-STYLE SMOKED PORK SPRING ROLLS

MAKES 30

1   cup smoked pork, fried and chopped
2   cups chopped bean sprouts
½   cup diced red bell pepper
1   cup sliced scallions
½   cup chopped cilantro

6   eggs
1   cup oyster sauce
2   Tbsp. minced garlic
2   Tbsp. grated ginger
Salt and pepper to taste

1   pkg. (16 oz.) spring roll wrappers (30 wrappers)
Egg wash
Oil for deep-frying

Combine smoked pork, bean sprouts, bell pepper, scallions, cilantro, eggs, oyster sauce, garlic, ginger, salt and pepper; blend well and let stand 15 minutes ⁊ Drain all liquid from mixture by squeezing in a towel ⁊ Stack spring roll wrappers on a work surface and cover with a damp towel ⁊ Place a wrapper with one corner facing you and spoon 2 tablespoons of the mixture about 2 inches from the front corner ⁊ Shape the filling into a long roll ⁊ Fold the front corner over the filling and roll upwards one turn to completely cover filling ⁊ Moisten the left and right corners with egg wash, fold in corners, and press down firmly to seal ⁊ Moisten the top corner with egg wash and roll into a cylinder ⁊ Set aside and complete remaining spring rolls ⁊ Deep-fry until crisp and golden brown, approximately 2 minutes ⁊ Drain on absorbent paper towels and serve immediately.

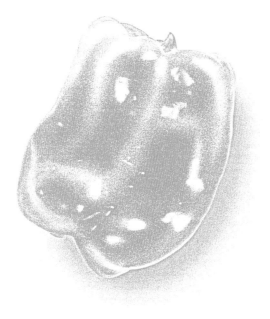

GREG GASPAR | THE WESTIN MAUI PRINCE HOTEL MAKENA

HAWAIIAN SPINY TAIL LOBSTER DUMPLINGS

With Tomato Herb Compote, Ginger Lime Butter Sauce and Balsamic Vinegar Reduction

SERVES 4

1 lb. fresh lobster meat, shelled and uncooked	10 oz. heavy cream	Tomato Herb Compote (see recipe below)
¼ tsp. salt	16 wonton wrappers (2-inch diameter)	Balsamic Vinegar Reduction (see recipe below)
¼ tsp. white pepper	Egg wash	
3 Tbsp. finely chopped shallots	Ginger Lime Butter Sauce (see recipe below)	
4 egg whites		

In a food processor cut lobster meat into small pieces ❧ Add salt, white pepper, shallots and egg whites ❧ Purée for one minute ❧ Slowly add heavy cream while processing ❧ Remove mixture from processor ❧ Place wrappers on a cutting board ❧ Place one ounce lobster mousse in each wrapper and paint edge of wrapper with egg wash and seal ❧ Place in refrigerator ❧ When ready for service, poach dumplings in pot of simmering, lightly salted water for 2 to 3 minutes or until cooked ❧ Remove from water ❧ Place on dry cloth ❧ Place Ginger Lime Butter Sauce on plate ❧ Top with four dumplings and place Tomato Herb Compote in center of dumplings ❧ Drizzle with Balsamic Vinegar Reduction over dumplings and serve.

GINGER LIME BUTTER SAUCE

¾ cup white wine	2 Tbsp. chopped ginger	12 oz. unsalted butter
3 Tbsp. chopped shallots	4 Tbsp. heavy cream	Salt and pepper to taste

In a heavy sauce pot combine all ingredients, except heavy cream and butter ❧ Cook until mixture is reduced by half ❧ Add heavy cream and reduce by half ❧ Slowly add butter ❧ Season with salt and pepper.

TOMATO HERB COMPOTE

1 cup diced tomato	½ tsp. chopped fresh thyme	2 tsp. olive oil
½ tsp. chopped fresh parsley	½ tsp. chopped fresh chervil	Salt and pepper to taste

Sauté tomato and fresh herbs in olive oil ❧ Season to taste.

BALSAMIC VINEGAR REDUCTION

8 oz. balsamic vinegar

Place vinegar in a heavy sauce pot ❧ Reduce over medium heat by ⅔ volume (until syrup consistency) ❧ Let cool and set aside.

HAWAIIAN-STYLE CEVICHE

SERVES 4

8 oz. raw fish, preferably
   snapper or moi
½ cup sugar
½ cup soy sauce

¼ cup rice wine vinegar
¾ cup lime juice
½ tsp. minced garlic

1 oz. ginger, smashed
1 oz. wasabi paste
Sushi rice

Cut fish into 2-ounce slices. In a bowl combine sugar, soy sauce, rice wine vinegar, lime juice, garlic, ginger and wasabi paste. Add fish and marinate in the refrigerator for one hour. When ready to serve, place 2 slices of fish atop an individual portion of sushi rice. Spoon marinade over fish and rice.

HOT CALIFORNIA ROLLS

With Kona Lobster Mousse ... But with No Rice!

Romeo S. Collado

SERVES 4

Lobster Mousse (see recipe below)
2   Tbsp. Aioli (see recipe on next page)
1   Tbsp. Chile Pepper Aioli (see recipe on next page)
Soy Mustard (see recipe on next page)
2   oz. cooked Dungeness crabmeat (about ½ cup)
1   tsp. cayenne
1   tsp. freshly squeezed lemon juice

½   cup fresh corn kernels (from 1 ear corn)
½   avocado, diced
3   sheets nori (8-inch squares)
Tarragon Vinaigrette (see recipe on next page)
Garnish:
4   Tbsp. salmon caviar
4   Tbsp. wasabi tobiko
Mixed salad greens

Prepare Lobster Mousse, Aioli and Chile Pepper Aioli and refrigerate until needed ❧ Prepare Soy Mustard and set aside ❧ In a mixing bowl combine crabmeat, Aioli, cayenne, lemon juice, corn and avocado.

Cut one nori sheet in half lengthwise and place on a work surface ❧ Spread the crab mixture in a line across the long side and roll up ❧ Place a full nori sheet on a work surface ❧ Spread with an even layer of the mousse ❧ Place the crab roll on top of the mousse and roll up ❧ Repeat this process with the remaining half and full nori sheets ❧ Wrap both rolls in plastic wrap and chill in the refrigerator for 15 minutes to firm the mixture and facilitate handling ❧ Preheat oven to 350°F ❧ Slice each roll into 6 pieces ❧ Place a pearl-sized amount of the Chile Pepper Aioli at the top of each slice ❧ Transfer the slices to a lightly oiled nonstick baking sheet and bake for 8 to 10 minutes or until the mousse is cooked through ❧ To serve, arrange 3 slices of the California Rolls on each plate and drizzle with the Soy Mustard ❧ Pour the Tarragon Vinaigrette around each plate ❧ Garnish with the salmon caviar, wasabi tobiko and mixed salad greens.

Traditionally, Asian-style California rolls are made with rice, crab and avocado wrapped inside a sheet of nori. This version replaces the rice with a traditional French-style lobster mousse—another successful example of East meeting West. One other departure here is that these rolls are served hot. You might want to prepare the Aioli (page 29) first as it is used both in the mousse and as the base for the Chile Pepper Aioli that is used as a garnish. Store the excess dressing in the refrigerator for up to 1 week; shake well before using. (Note: Recipes containing raw eggs are not recommended for immuno-compromised individuals or small children.)

LOBSTER MOUSSE

1   tsp. butter
1   shallot, minced

4   fresh uncooked lobster tails (about 4 oz. each), shelled and chopped

1   egg white
Salt to taste
1¼ cups heavy cream

ALAN WONG | ALAN WONG'S RESTAURANT

To prepare the mousse, in a small sauté pan over medium heat, melt the butter ❧ Add the shallot and sweat for about 45 seconds, or until translucent ❧ Let cool and transfer to a food processor ❧ Add the lobster, egg white and salt and purée until smooth ❧ With the machine running, slowly add the cream in a steady stream until fully incorporated; do not overmix ❧ Refrigerate until needed.

AIOLI

YIELDS 1½ CUPS

1 tsp. Dijon mustard	1 Tbsp. freshly squeezed lemon juice	1 cup olive oil
1 tsp. minced garlic		Salt and pepper to taste
1 egg plus 1 yolk		

In a blender, combine the mustard, garlic, egg, egg yolk and lemon juice and purée ❧ With the machine running, slowly add the olive oil until incorporated ❧ If the mixture becomes too thick, thin with a little water ❧ Season with salt and pepper ❧ Keep refrigerated.

CHILE PEPPER AIOLI

YIELDS ¼ CUP

¼ cup Aioli
⅛ tsp. cayenne, or to taste

In a bowl, thoroughly combine the Aioli and cayenne ❧ Keep refrigerated.

SOY MUSTARD

1½ Tbsp. mustard powder
1½ Tbsp. warm water
1 Tbsp. soy sauce

In a bowl combine mustard powder and water to form a smooth paste ❧ Stir in the soy sauce ❧ Set aside.

TARRAGON VINAIGRETTE

1 egg	2 tsp. minced garlic	Salt to taste
1 Tbsp. Dijon mustard	2 tsp. minced shallots	Up to ¼ cup water
¼ cup plus 2 Tbsp. tarragon vinegar	2 cups olive oil	¼ cup tobiko

In a blender combine egg, Dijon mustard, tarragon vinegar, garlic and shallots and purée ❧ With the machine running, add the olive oil and blend until incorporated ❧ Season with salt ❧ If the mixture becomes too stiff, add the water, a little at a time, until the desired consistency is reached ❧ The vinaigrette should be pourable ❧ Stir in the tobiko.

Chef suggestion: Use Yamasa brand soy sauce.

ISLAND PORK TOSTADAS

With Pineapple Salsa

SERVES 4

4 flour tortillas	2 oz. goat cheese, crumbled	Pineapple Salsa
¼ cup hoisin sauce	8 oz. warm cooked pork,	(see recipe below)
Black Beans (see recipe below)	shredded (about 1 cup)	

Preheat oven to 400°F. Place tortillas directly on middle oven rack and cook until warm. Place tortillas on serving plates and brush with hoisin sauce. Top each with ½ cup Black Beans, 2 tablespoons of the goat cheese, ¼ cup of the pork and ½ cup of the Pineapple Salsa.

BLACK BEANS

1 Tbsp. vegetable oil	1 can (16 oz.) black beans,	2 Tbsp. water
½ cup chopped red bell pepper	rinsed and drained	2 tsp. Chinese five-spice powder
½ cup chopped onion	1 jalapeno pepper, finely	¼ tsp. salt and pepper
½ tsp. minced garlic	chopped	

Heat oil in a large nonstick skillet. Add bell pepper, onion and garlic and cook over medium heat for 3 to 4 minutes, stirring occasionally, until tender. Stir in the remaining ingredients and cook over low heat for 3 to 4 minutes for flavors to blend.

PINEAPPLE SALSA

1½ cups diced fresh pineapple	¼ cup thinly sliced scallions	1½ Tbsp. fresh lime juice
½ cup finely chopped red bell pepper	2 Tbsp. chopped cilantro	1½ tsp. vegetable oil

In a bowl combine all ingredients and blend well.

KĀLUA DUCKLING POT STICKERS

With Roasted Waimea Corn and Tomato Salsa

SERVES 6

12 oz. duck meat (leg meat, cooked kālua style)	18 mandoo or wonton wrappers
1 oz. Hāmākua goat cheese	1 Tbsp. olive oil (to cook the pot stickers)
1 Tbsp. chopped green onions	Roasted Waimea Corn and Tomato Salsa (see recipe below)
1 Tbsp. chopped ginger	
1 oz. garlic, roasted and chopped	Whole sprigs of green onion and lemongrass for garnish
Salt and pepper to taste	

Shred duck meat.◆ In a large bowl, combine duck meat, goat cheese, green onions, ginger and garlic; toss to mix.◆ Season to taste with salt and pepper.◆ Make certain that the mixture is a little soft, and if needed, add a touch of cream or milk to soften.◆ Form the pot stickers in a half-moon shape.◆ Remember to moisten the wonton wrappers before closing them.◆ Steam the pot stickers lightly, then sauté in hot oil.◆ Make sure the bottom is brown and crispy when serving.◆ Serve 3 pieces per appetizer in a small Chinese steamer with the Roasted Waimea Corn and Tomato Salsa in a ramekin.◆ Garnish with whole sprigs of green onion and lemongrass for a dramatic presentation.

ROASTED WAIMEA CORN AND TOMATO SALSA

2 Kamuela tomatoes	Salt and pepper to taste	1 Tbsp. chopped cilantro
2 Tbsp. extra virgin olive oil	1 red onion, diced	1 Tbsp. rice vinegar
1 clove garlic, minced	2 Tbsp. lemongrass water*	½ tsp. cumin powder, roasted
1 Tbsp. minced fresh herbs (chervil, basil, mint)	1 Tbsp. honey (Hilo tropical flower preferred)	
1 ear of corn		

Cut tomatoes in half and rub with 1 tablespoon of the olive oil, garlic and fresh herbs.◆ Roast in a 300°F oven until cooked.◆ Set aside and dice when cool.◆ Rub corn with part of the olive oil and season with salt and pepper, then slow roast in the oven until cooked.◆ Cut off the kernels.◆ In a bowl combine diced roasted tomatoes, corn kernels and red onion.◆ Stir in lemongrass water, honey, cilantro, rice vinegar, the remaining olive oil, cumin powder, salt and pepper; blend well.

Chef's Suggestion: If you are not able to use kālua duck, use roasted duck or smoked duck meat.

*Lemongrass water—Simmer lemongrass stalks in water for 10 minutes, then reserve.

KĀLUA PIG AND GOAT CHEESE QUESADILLA

SERVES 6

¼ cup julienne Poblano or Anaheim chili	½ cup goat cheese	6 flour tortillas
½ cup julienne red bell pepper	2 Tbsp. minced fresh ginger	Plum Papaya Dipping Sauce (see recipe below)
1 Tbsp. vegetable oil	2 Tbsp. minced fresh cilantro	
1 cup Oven Kālua Pig, shredded (see recipe below)	½ cup julienne Bermuda onion	

Sauté chili and red bell pepper in oil until wilted ❧ Cool ❧ Add all the remaining ingredients, except tortillas and plum sauce, and mix well ❧ Divide the kālua pig mixture into six portions and place one portion on each tortilla ❧ Spread the filling over one half of the tortilla and carefully close ❧ Brush lightly with oil and grill until filling is hot, about 1½ minutes per side ❧ Cut into quarters and serve with Plum Papaya Dipping Sauce.

OVEN KĀLUA PIG

MAKES 5-6 CUPS

4 to 5 lb. pork butt	1 tsp. liquid smoke
Banana or ti leaves	Water
3 Tbsp. sea salt	

Line a roasting pan with ti or banana leaves ❧ Cut the pork butt into 1"x1"x2" chunks and place in the pan ❧ Add the salt, liquid smoke and water to almost cover ❧ Cover pan with foil and bake at 375°F for 2 hours ❧ When done, pork will be very tender, and seem a bit salty ❧ Lift the pork out of the broth and discard the liquid ❧ When cool enough to handle, shred the meat and discard the excess fat ❧ Pork is ready to use in other preparations or as a sandwich with cabbage leaves and barbecue sauce.

PLUM PAPAYA DIPPING SAUCE

MAKES 3 CUPS

1 cup soft papaya pulp	1 tsp. minced garlic	½ cup thinly sliced green onions
1 cup Chinese plum sauce	1 tsp. chopped shallot	½ tsp. salt
⅓ cup rice vinegar	2 tsp. minced ginger	½ cup vegetable oil

Combine all ingredients, except oil, in a food processor ❧ Purée until smooth, then slowly add oil.

SCOTT LUTEY | SHERATON KAUA'I RESORT

KAUA'I PRAWNS STUFFED WITH 'AHI POKE

SERVES 4

6   oz. finely diced 'ahi
2   Tbsp. minced Maui onion
3   Tbsp. chopped ogo
1   tsp. sesame oil
½   tsp. sesame seeds
1   tsp. inamona (roasted
      kukui nuts)
Chili paste to taste

Alae salt (red sea salt) to taste
8   Kaua'i prawns, shelled and
      deveined
½   cup all-purpose flour
¼   cup cornstarch
1   egg
½   cup water
1   lb. sweet potato strings

Garnish:
1   cup wild greens
Sweet Chili Sauce (see recipe below)
1   Tbsp. slivered green onion
1   Tbsp. orange tobiko (flying fish
      eggs)
1   Tbsp. black tobiko (flying fish
      eggs)
1   tsp. black sesame seeds

In a bowl combine 'ahi, onion, ogo, sesame oil, sesame seeds and inamona; mix well. Season to taste with chili paste and alae salt. Preheat oil for deep-frying to 350°F. Stuff shrimp with 'ahi poke mixture. Prepare tempura batter by combining flour, cornstarch, egg and water; blend well. Roll shrimp in tempura batter. Wrap shrimp with sweet potato strings. Fry shrimp for 1 to 2 minutes. Place wild greens in center of plate and arrange 2 shrimp around plate. Drizzle Sweet Chili Sauce around plate and garnish with tobiko and sesame seeds.

SWEET CHILI SAUCE

2   Tbsp. chili paste
1   cup honey

Juice of 2 limes
½   cup ketchup

In a bowl combine all ingredients and whisk together. Reserve until ready to serve.

Chef's Suggestion: You can substitute roasted macadamia nuts for the kukui nuts and kosher salt for the alae salt.

GREG GASPAR | THE WESTIN MAUI PRINCE HOTEL MAKENA

KONA LOBSTER AND ROCK SHRIMP CAKE

With Warm Tomato Vinaigrette and Shiitake Mushroom Poke

SERVES 4

½	lb. Kona lobster meat	1	tsp. chopped fresh thyme		Salt and white pepper to taste
¼	lb. rock shrimp	2	egg whites		Warm Tomato Vinaigrette (see
4	cups fish stock	1	egg yolk		recipe below)
2	Tbsp. diced red bell pepper	2	Tbsp. heavy cream		Shiitake Mushroom Poke (see
2	Tbsp. diced Maui onion	10	oz. dried bread crumbs		recipe below)
1	tsp. chopped parsley	2	Tbsp. olive oil		

Poach lobster meat and rock shrimp in fish stock for 90 seconds; let cool ✦ In a medium-size bowl shred lobster meat and rock shrimp ✦ Add bell pepper, onion and herbs and mix together ✦ Add eggs, heavy cream and bread crumbs and mix together ✦ Form into small cakes ✦ Heat olive oil in a sauté pan over medium heat ✦ Fry cakes for 2 to 3 minutes until golden brown on each side ✦ Remove from sauté pan and place on paper towel to drain oil ✦ Place tomato vinaigrette on center of plate, add cakes, and place mushroom mixture on top of cakes.

WARM TOMATO VINAIGRETTE

4	Tbsp. olive oil	2	cups tomato water or juice
2	large tomatoes, skinned, diced	2	Tbsp. balsamic vinegar
	and seeded	1	Tbsp. chopped fresh cilantro
2	tsp. minced shallots		Salt and white pepper to taste

In medium sauté pan, on high heat, add 1 tablespoon olive oil, tomatoes and shallots ✦ Add tomato water, 3 tablespoons of olive oil and balsamic vinegar ✦ Add cilantro and season to taste.

SHIITAKE MUSHROOM POKE

½	lb. shiitake mushrooms, sliced	¼	cup chopped green onion	2	tsp. light soy sauce
1½	cups fish stock	¼	cup chopped red and green	1	tsp. Hawaiian salt
	Salt and white pepper to taste		ogo (seaweed)	½	tsp. diced Hawaiian red chili
¼	cup julienne tomato, seeded	3	tsp. chopped garlic		pepper
¼	cup julienne Maui onion	3	tsp. chopped ginger		

In a medium saucepan sauté shiitake mushrooms in fish stock ✦ Season to taste with salt and pepper; set aside to cool ✦ Combine mushrooms with tomato, Maui onion, green onion, seaweed, garlic, ginger, soy sauce, Hawaiian salt and Hawaiian red chili pepper; mix well.

KONA LOBSTER-CRAB CAKES

With Spiced Mustard Sauce and Avocado Relish

SERVES 4

8 oz. lobster meat	1 tsp. chopped chives	1 qt. vegetable oil for frying
8 oz. Kona crabmeat (you may substitute Dungeness crab)	½ Tbsp. chopped shallot	Spiced Mustard Sauce (see recipe below)
4 oz. scallops, well rinsed	4-8 sprigs fresh chervil	Avocado Relish (see recipe below)
1 Tbsp. chopped garlic	1 large egg	
1 Tbsp. chopped cilantro	2½ cups panko flakes	Garnish: chervil sprigs or chopped chives
1 tsp. chopped parsley	2 Tbsp. heavy cream	
	Salt and white pepper to taste	

In a large food processor combine half of the lobster, half of the crab, the scallops, garlic, cilantro, parsley, chives, shallot, chervil, egg and ½ cup of the panko flakes; purée ❧ Remove mixture and place in a large bowl ❧ Dice the remaining lobster and crab and, using a rubber spatula, fold it into the mixture ❧ Then fold in the heavy cream ❧ Season to taste with salt and white pepper ❧ Keep mixture chilled until just before serving ❧ In a saucepan heat oil over medium-high heat ❧ Divide cake mixture into four large or eight smaller portions ❧ Shape portions into disks and roll in reserved panko flakes ❧ Gently fry until golden brown and crisp on the outside ❧ You may want to bake in a 350°F oven for three minutes to ensure center is hot ❧ Place a small dollop of Spiced Mustard Sauce on a decorative salad plate ❧ Place the cooked cake on the sauce and top with a large spoonful of Avocado Relish ❧ Garnish with chervil sprigs or chopped chives.

SPICED MUSTARD SAUCE

½ cup Dijon mustard	2 Tbsp. rice wine vinegar	1 Tbsp. sugar
3 Tbsp. yellow powdered mustard	1 tsp. chopped garlic	¼ cup salad oil
	2 tsp. tamari	Warm water

Place all ingredients, except oil and warm water, in a blender or food processor ❧ Mix on high speed and slowly add the oil until sauce is thick and shiny ❧ Add warm water, if needed for thinning.

AVOCADO RELISH

1 cup ripe avocado, skin removed and diced	1 Tbsp. chopped cilantro	Kosher salt to taste
1 oz. red onion, diced	1 Tbsp. chopped garlic	Ground pepper to taste
	Juice of ½ lime	2 Tbsp. crème fraîche

In a large mixing bowl combine all ingredients, except crème fraîche; blend well ❧ Fold in crème fraîche and refrigerate.

DAVID BOUCHER | HYATT REGENCY KAUA'I

LOCAL-STYLE 'AHI POKE

On Togarashi Scallops and Hanalei Sweet Potato Cake

SERVES 3

Dana Edmunds

TOGARASHI-SPICED SCALLOPS

3	fresh jumbo scallops	1	tsp. thinly sliced green
Togarashi spice to taste			onion
8	oz. 'ahi block, diced	1	Tbsp. chopped onion
⅛	tsp. Hawaiian salt	1	tsp. chopped garlic
⅛	tsp. minced kukui nut	1	Tbsp. furikake spice
¼	tsp. brown sugar	1	Tbsp. sesame oil
Pinch of chili flakes		Hanalei Sweet Potato Cake	
1	tsp. soy sauce		(see recipe below)
1	tsp. oyster sauce		

Prepare the day of use. Season scallops to taste with togarashi and sear when ready to serve. Combine all the remaining ingredients, except sweet potato cake, in a stainless steel bowl and mix gently. Place a sweet potato cake on a plate. Top with a scallop and a scoop of poke.

HANALEI SWEET POTATO CAKE

1	russet potato	1	Tbsp. minced ginger	Salt and pepper to taste
1	Hanalei or Okinawan sweet	1	Tbsp. minced garlic	1 egg
	potato	2	Tbsp. chopped cilantro	

Grate the potato and sweet potato. Bring a large saucepan of water to a boil and blanch for 2 minutes. Cool in an ice bath. Stir in ginger, garlic, cilantro, salt and pepper. Add egg and mix well. Heat a sauté pan and add a small amount of oil. Place a scoop of potato mixture into pan and flatten with a spatula. Cook until golden brown.

LOLLIPOP OF CRISPY SHRIMP

With Maui Sugarcane Dipping Sauce

SERVES 4

8 ocean prawns, heads on	1 oz. heavy cream	4 sheets lumpia wrapper
2 bulbs garlic	1 oz. chopped water chestnuts	4 oz. flour for dusting
4 oz. Chinese bay scallops	Japanese 7-spice blend to taste	2 eggs, well beaten
1 shallot, minced	Juice of 1 lemon	8 oz. oil for sautéing
3 Tbsp. oil	8 oz. panko	Maui Sugarcane Dipping Sauce
1 oz. white wine	2 oz. furikake	(see recipe below)

Clean and butterfly prawns, leaving heads on ❧ Remove the veins and rinse, then pat dry with a clean paper towel ❧ Poach garlic in chicken stock, until soft enough to purée ❧ Prepare mousse in a buffalo chopper or blender by grinding bay scallops until smooth and creamy ❧ In a separate pan sauté shallot in oil until transparent ❧ Add white wine and reduce by half ❧ Finish with heavy cream and reduce by half ❧ Fold this reduction into the scallop mixture ❧ Stir in garlic purée and water chestnuts ❧ Complete by seasoning with Japanese 7-spice blend and lemon juice ❧ Pipe approximately ¼ ounce of mousse into each shrimp ❧ Combine panko and furikake ❧ Wrap entire tail of shrimp with lumpia wrapper ❧ Dust in flour, dip in egg, and roll in panko mixture ❧ Sauté in oil on both sides until finished and golden brown ❧ Prepare Maui Sugarcane Dipping Sauce ❧ Garnish plate and serve shrimp with salad of your choice ❧ Drizzle sauce on top of shrimp and serve.

MAUI SUGARCANE DIPPING SAUCE

2 sticks Maui sugarcane, peeled and chopped	1 Hawaiian chili pepper, finely minced	2 stalks lemongrass, crushed
4 oz. water	1 oz. simple syrup	1 Tbsp. cornstarch
		2 Tbsp. water

In a small saucepan combine sugarcane, the 4 ounces of water and chili pepper; simmer ❧ Be sure to add chili pepper a little at a time to adjust the heat ❧ Stir in simple syrup and lemongrass ❧ Dissolve cornstarch in the 2 tablespoons of water ❧ Bring sugarcane mixture to a boil and slowly stir in cornstarch mixture ❧ Reduce heat and cook until thickened ❧ Strain and reserve sauce.

ALAN TSUCHIYAMA | SHERATON WAIKĪKĪ

MACADAMIA NUT HUMMUS

YIELDS 2½ CUPS

½   cup roasted macadamia nuts
2   cups garbanzo beans, drained
2   Tbsp. olive oil

1   Tbsp. lemon juice
3   Tbsp. water
1   tsp. minced garlic

10   medium basil leaves
Salt and pepper to taste

In a food processor combine all ingredients and purée. Serve as a spread on lavosh or thinly sliced bread, or as a dip for vegetables.

PACIFIC SAMPLER

CHARRED 'AHI POKE

SERVES 8

6   oz. 'ahi block

1   Tbsp. Cajun seasoning

1¾ oz. Maui onion, chopped

1¾ oz. green onion, chopped

1   Tbsp. chopped kukui nuts

1¾ oz. red ogo, chopped

2   Tbsp. sesame oil

1   Tbsp. alae salt

Roll 'ahi block in Cajun seasoning and char on the outside at very high heat in a cast-iron skillet. Chill, then dice into ¼" cubes. In a mixing bowl combine 'ahi and all the remaining ingredients; mix well. Adjust seasoning and chill until ready to serve.

HAMACHI SHOOTER

SERVES 10

2⅝ oz. yellowtail filet (sashimi grade), thinly sliced	5⅞ oz. tomato juice	⅛ oz. Tabasco sauce
¾ Tbsp. lime juice	1½ oz. passion fruit syrup	½ tsp. cracked black pepper
½ tsp. sea salt	1½ oz. orange juice	1½ oz. vodka

Thinly slice the yellowtail filet. Spray with lime juice and sprinkle with sea salt. Let rest in refrigerator until ready to serve. Mix together tomato juice, passion fruit syrup, orange juice, Tabasco sauce, black pepper and vodka; blend well. Place 2 cured fish slices into each shooter glass and top off with tomato mixture. Serve immediately.

LOBSTER COCKTAIL

SERVES 10

8 oz. tomato juice	7 oz. mango, ripe and finely diced	⅜ tsp. freshly ground black pepper
3 oz. sweet chili sauce	½ oz. cilantro, chopped	10 oz. cooked lobster meat, diced
¾ oz. lime juice	⅛ Tbsp. Kosher salt	
¾ oz. lemon juice		

Combine all ingredients; blend well and adjust seasoning. Chill until ready to serve.

POISSON CRU

SERVES 7

4 oz. red snapper filet	2 Tbsp. coconut milk	¼ cup diced cucumber
¼ cup lime juice	¼ cup diced tomato	¼ cup chopped green onions
½ Tbsp. sea salt	¼ cup diced Maui onions	

Thinly slice fish filet and marinate with lime juice and sea salt; set aside until the fish turns opaque. Drain fish and add all remaining ingredients; adjust seasoning and serve chilled.

PACIFIC RIM SUSHI

SERVES 8

Oil for deep-frying
8   oz. snow crabmeat
1   Tbsp. mayonnaise
4   sheets nori (dried seaweed wrap)
Cooked white rice
2   avocadoes, peeled, seeded and sliced

2   cups tempura flour
1½ cups ice water
1   cup toasted, diced macadamia nuts
2   cups panko (Japanese bread crumbs)

1   cup wild greens
Thai Curry Sauce (see recipe below)
2   Tbsp. black sesame seeds
2   Tbsp. red tobiko

Preheat oil to 350°F ❧ In a small bowl mix crabmeat and mayonnaise ❧ Place a sheet of nori on a sushi mat ❧ Spread rice along lower edge of nori, about 2 inches thick ❧ Arrange 2 tablespoons of crabmeat and 2 slices of avocado lengthwise in the middle of the white rice ❧ Roll up the nori tightly and seal edges with water ❧ In a bowl whisk together tempura flour and ice water ❧ Combine macadamia nuts and panko on a plate ❧ Dip sushi in tempura batter and roll in macadamia crust ❧ Deep-fry sushi until golden brown ❧ Remove and drain on absorbent paper ❧ Slice each sushi roll into 6 portions ❧ Place wild greens in middle of plate and drizzle with Thai Curry Sauce ❧ Arrange 3 slices of sushi around wild greens ❧ Garnish with black sesame seeds and tobiko.

THAI CURRY SAUCE

SERVES 4

1½ Tbsp. sesame oil
1   Tbsp. chopped ginger
1   tsp. minced garlic

1   tsp. Thai red curry paste (Mae Ploy brand)
1   cup coconut syrup

1   cup heavy cream
½   lb. unsalted butter

In a sauce pot heat sesame oil ❧ Add ginger, garlic and Thai curry paste and sauté for 1 minute ❧ Add coconut syrup and heavy cream and simmer until sauce coats the back of the spoon ❧ Remove from heat; whip in butter and strain through a fine sieve ❧ Reserve in a warm area.

JAMES McDONALD | I'O

Pan Asian Rockefeller

SERVES 6

2	Tbsp. smoked bacon, diced	2	cups Coconut Cream (see recipe below)	½	cup minced green onions
½	lb. fresh spinach	1½	cups Herb Topping (see recipe below)	2	Tbsp. tobiko caviar
2	Tbsp. minced shallots			Salt and pepper to taste	
30	oysters, removed from shell, liquid reserved				

Sauté bacon briefly in hot pan until lightly browned ❧ Add spinach and shallots and cook until just wilted ❧ Place mixture in six ovenproof dishes ❧ Place five oysters in each dish and cover with Coconut Cream ❧ Bake at 425°F for three to four minutes ❧ Sprinkle with Herb Topping and brown under broiler ❧ Mix green onions with tobiko and garnish on top of oysters ❧ Serve immediately.

COCONUT CREAM

1	Tbsp. butter	½	tsp. brown sugar	1	cup coconut milk
1	Tbsp. flour	1	oz. Pernod	1	tsp. fresh lemon juice
⅛	tsp. curry powder		Reserved oyster liquid	Salt and pepper to taste	
1	star anise	½	cup clam juice		

In a saucepan melt butter over medium heat ❧ Add flour and cook to form a roux ❧ Add curry, star anise and brown sugar and continue to stir ❧ Add Pernod, oyster liquid, clam juice and coconut milk ❧ Bring to a boil, whisking constantly ❧ Lower heat and simmer for 15 minutes ❧ Add lemon juice and season to taste.

HERB TOPPING

1½	cups panko flakes	½	cup grated Parmesan cheese
1	Tbsp. mixed dry herbs	2	oz. olive oil

Combine all ingredients; mix well and set aside in refrigerator.

PANCETTA-WRAPPED SHRIMP

With Roasted Red Pepper Aioli

SERVES 4

16 shrimp (21-25 count), peeled and deveined with the tail left on

Salt and pepper to taste

16 slices pancetta or gourmet smoked bacon

Roasted Red Pepper Aioli (see recipe below)

Parsley for garnish

Season shrimp with salt and pepper. Wrap each shrimp with the pancetta, starting from the head end of the shrimp, making sure to overlap each layer. Heat a sauté pan over medium heat and fry the shrimp until each side of the pancetta becomes rendered and crispy. When this is completed the shrimp inside will be cooked. Place shrimp on absorbent paper and then onto a serving plate. Top with a dollop of Roasted Red Pepper Aioli and garnish with parsley.

ROASTED RED PEPPER AIOLI

1 red bell pepper

1 egg yolk

¼ tsp. chopped garlic

½ cup vegetable oil

Salt and pepper to taste

Over an open flame, roast the bell pepper, turning occasionally until all sides are charred. Place the bell pepper on a plate and cover with plastic wrap until cool. Rub off the charred skin and remove the stem, seeds and ribs. With a cook's knife, chop until fine and set aside. In a small nonreactive bowl and using a small wire whip, whisk together the egg yolk and garlic. Slowly drizzle in the oil, until it becomes thick (the oil will emulsify in the yolk and produce a mayonnaise). Stir in the chopped bell pepper and season with salt and pepper.

RUSSELL SIU | 3660 ON THE RISE

Ric Noyle

PANKO-CRUSTED 'AHI SASHIMI

With Soy Wasabi Butter Sauce

MAKES 1 ROLL

1 sheet nori
1 oz. rice
1 oz. fresh arugula or spinach
5 oz. fresh sashimi-grade 'ahi
   (or use salmon, crab,
   vegetables or combinations)

Salt to taste
4 oz. tempura batter
4 oz. panko flakes
Soy Wasabi Butter Sauce (see
   recipe below)

Black sesame seeds
Chives, chopped
Oil for deep-frying

On the top 1" of the nori, spread the rice about 2 grains high ❧ Lay the arugula on the bottom third of the nori ❧ Place the 'ahi on the arugula ❧ Season with salt ❧ Roll tight with a sushi rolling mat ❧ Dip in tempura batter ❧ Roll in panko flakes and set aside ❧ Sauce the serving plate with the Soy Wasabi Butter Sauce and sprinkle with black sesame seeds and chives ❧ Fry the roll until the panko coating is light golden brown ❧ Slice roll and arrange on plate ❧ Enjoy!

SOY WASABI BUTTER SAUCE

1 tsp. chopped shallots
3 oz. white wine

1 tsp. rice wine vinegar
¼ lb. unsalted butter

3 oz. soy sauce
1 tsp. wasabi paste

Sauté shallots and add wine and vinegar; reduce by half ❧ Whip butter into reduction and strain ❧ Mix soy sauce and wasabi paste together and whip into butter sauce.

Steve Brinkman

PINEAPPLE CILANTRO SALSA

MAKES 4 CUPS

1   ripe pineapple, peeled, cored and diced

2   small jalapeno peppers, seeds removed and diced

½   red bell pepper, diced

½   green bell pepper, diced

1   small red onion, diced

4   Tbsp. chopped cilantro

2   Tbsp. chopped garlic

½   cup olive oil

Juice of 1 lemon

Salt and pepper to taste

Combine all ingredients and mix well. Serve over fresh Island fish. Enjoy!

PINEAPPLE TOMATILLO SALSA

MAKES ¾ CUP

¼ cup fresh diced pineapple	1 Tbsp. chopped fresh ginger	3 Tbsp. chopped cilantro
¼ cup tomatillo purée	1 tsp. Hawaiian sea salt	1 chili pepper, diced
Juice of 2 limes	½ tsp. freshly ground black	1 Tbsp. chopped fresh mint
3 cloves garlic	pepper	

In a bowl combine pineapple, tomatillo purée, lime juice, garlic, ginger, salt and pepper; mix well ⁂ Place ½ cup of the mixture at a time in a blender and purée for 15 seconds or until smooth ⁂ Continue processing, until all is puréed ⁂ Stir in cilantro, chili pepper and mint ⁂ Serve with tacos or with grilled chicken.

"POKY PINES"

Crispy 'Ahi Poke with Avocado, Wasabi Soy Sauce, Togarashi Aioli, and Tarragon Vinaigrette

SERVES 4

½ cup Aioli (page 29)
½ Tbsp. shichimi togarashi
1 tsp. red wine vinegar
8 square wonton wrappers
Cornstarch for sprinkling
1 cup 'Ahi Poke (see recipe below)
Vegetable oil for deep-frying

1 avocado, peeled, pitted and halved
¼ cup Tarragon Vinaigrette (page 29)
Wasabi Soy Sauce (see recipe on next page)
4 amaranth leaves or watercress sprigs for garnish

In a bowl combine the Aioli, shichimi togarashi and vinegar; blend well ❧ Refrigerate until needed ❧ On a flat work surface, stack the wrappers, sprinkling a little cornstarch between each one so they do not stick ❧ Cut into long, thin strips and divide into 8 even piles ❧ Using your hands, shape the poke into 8 compact, golf ball-sized balls ❧ Press one side of the strips around the outside of a poke ball with the ends sticking upright ❧ Repeat for the remaining poke strips ❧ In a deep fryer or large saucepan over high heat, heat about 3 inches of vegetable oil to 350°F ❧ Using tongs or chopsticks, gently lower the "poky pines", one at a time, into the hot oil ❧ Keeping them upright, deep-fry about 45 seconds or until golden brown ❧ Remove and drain on paper towels ❧ Quarter each avocado half, thinly slice to form a fan, and arrange on individual plates ❧ Place two dollops of the Aioli in the center of each plate and put a "poky pine" on top of each dollop ❧ Drizzle the Tarragon Vinaigrette and Wasabi Soy Sauce around each plate ❧ Place an amaranth leaf or watercress sprig between the "poky pines".

The spiky centerpiece of this dish—poke deep-fried inside a wild-looking package of wonton strips—looks like a pair of hyper porcupines, hence the name. This recipe is a good example of how I create some of my dishes: I like to play with ingredients in the kitchen, and sometimes I feel like a child experimenting with his toys. If I like the way the flavors combine, and the whole dish makes sense, I look for a way to make an attractive presentation. In this case, I was experimenting with wrapping poke and noticed some deep-fried wonton strips we had on hand. These ingredients inspired this recipe, and I liked the strikingly unusual result. Fortunately, our guests at Alan Wong's feel the same way, and the "poky pines" are now a signature item on the menu.

'AHI POKE

12 oz. sashimi-grade 'ahi tuna, finely diced
½ cup Slivered Scallions (see recipe on next page)
½ cup minced white onion
2 Tbsp. chopped ogo (seaweed)
½ tsp. chili sauce with garlic (such as sambal olek)
1 tsp. dark sesame oil
½ tsp. inamona (optional)
½ tsp. rock salt
1 Tbsp. vegetable oil

To prepare the poke, in a bowl combine the tuna, scallions, onion, ogo, chili sauce, sesame oil, inamona and rock salt. Heat the vegetable oil in a sauté pan over high heat and sear the poke until browned on the outside but still rare in the middle, 30 to 40 seconds.

SLIVERED SCALLIONS

YIELDS ABOUT ¼ CUP

1   bunch of scallions, green parts only

Using the back of a large, sharp knife, flatten the green parts of the scallions. Cut very finely on a diagonal so that the slivers are about 1 inch long.

WASABI SOY SAUCE

2   Tbsp. wasabi powder
3   Tbsp. hot water
3   Tbsp. soy sauce

In a small bowl combine all ingredients and mix well. Refrigerate until needed.

Chef's Suggestion: Use Yamasa brand soy sauce.

Romeo S. Collado

SCOTT LUTEY | SHERATON KAUA'I RESORT

PROSCIUTTO-WRAPPED 'AHI

With Miso Vinaigrette

SERVES 4

4 'ahi blocks (2½ oz. each)	Oil for sautéing	Miso Vinaigrette (see recipe below)
4 spears asparagus, blanched	Cucumber Namasu (see recipe below)	½ cup sweet soy sauce
4 oz. Boursin cheese		Kaiware sprouts
½ lb. prosciutto, cut paper thin		

Slice 'ahi blocks in the center, ¾ the way down ❧ Place asparagus and Boursin cheese along center ❧ Press 'ahi together ❧ Place 'ahi on sliced prosciutto and roll tightly ❧ Heat a sauté pan over high heat and add enough oil to coat pan; sear 'ahi on both sides until prosciutto is crisp ❧ Place Cucumber Namasu in the center of plate ❧ Slice 'ahi and arrange around plate ❧ Drizzle Miso Vinaigrette and sweet soy sauce around plate ❧ Garnish with kaiware sprouts.

CUCUMBER NAMASU

1 Japanese cucumber, peeled, seeded and sliced	½ cup fine julienne carrots	1 tsp. toasted sesame seeds
	2 Tbsp. sushi vinegar	Salt and pepper to taste

In a bowl combine cucumber, carrots, sushi vinegar and sesame seeds; mix well ❧ Season to taste with salt and pepper.

MISO VINAIGRETTE

½ cup sushi vinegar	¼ cup mirin	½ cup canola oil
2 Tbsp. white miso paste	1 Tbsp. soy sauce	Salt and pepper to taste
2 Tbsp. sesame oil	2 Tbsp. minced fresh ginger	

In a blender combine sushi vinegar, miso, sesame oil, mirin, soy sauce and ginger ❧ Blend on high and slowly add canola oil until smooth ❧ Season to taste with salt and pepper.

SESAME BEEF KABOBS

MAKES 12

1½ lbs. lean beef (sirloin, New York or rib eye)

2 Tbsp. brown sugar

1 Tbsp. sesame seeds

1 tsp. minced garlic

½ tsp. crushed chilies

3 Tbsp. Mountain Gold shoyu

Cut beef into strips ⅓"x1"x4" ❧ Combine all the remaining ingredients and marinate beef ❧ Thread beef strips on 12 skewers ❧ Grill or barbeque on both sides until done to your taste.

JAMES MCDONALD | I'O

SHRIMP WONTONS

With Spicy Sweet & Sour Sauce and Hawaiian Salsa

SERVES 6

Marinade (see recipe below)
24 large shrimp, peeled
24 wonton wrappers
24 leaves fresh basil
Oil for deep-frying
Sweet & Sour Sauce (see recipe below)

Hawaiian Salsa (see recipe below)
6 oz. hoisin sauce (in a squeeze bottle)

Pour Marinade over peeled shrimp and let stand 15 minutes. Lay wonton wrappers on a flat surface and place one basil leaf on each wrapper. Place one shrimp on each piece of basil. Roll wonton closed around the shrimp. Deep-fry at 350°F until wontons are crisp and shrimp is lightly cooked, about 1½ to 2 minutes. Arrange four wontons on each plate, ladle Sweet & Sour Sauce over the wontons, and top each with a spoonful of Hawaiian Salsa. Finish with a drizzle of hoisin.

MARINADE

1 cup low salt soy sauce
2 stalks lemongrass, chopped
1 cup sesame oil

2 bulbs ginger root, peeled
2 cloves garlic, peeled

1 cup loosely packed fresh cilantro
1 egg

In a blender combine all ingredients and process until smooth.

SWEET & SOUR SAUCE

1 cup sugar
1 tsp. red chili flakes

1 cup red wine
1 tsp. ground cinnamon

1 Tbsp. low salt soy sauce

In a saucepan combine all ingredients and simmer for 20 minutes.

HAWAIIAN SALSA

2 large ripe mangoes, peeled and diced small (you can substitute papaya or pineapple)

1 medium onion, peeled and diced small

½ cup loosely packed fresh cilantro, chopped

In a bowl combine all ingredients and mix gently.

54

JEFF WIND | HYATT REGENCY WAIKĪKĪ RESORT & SPA

SPICY SEAFOOD PIZZA

SERVES 4

1   cup bay shrimp, chopped
1   cup crabmeat, drained and
    broken into pieces

1   cup lobster meat, cooked and
    chopped
½   cup mayonnaise

3   Tbsp. shiracha chili sauce
4   thick flour tortillas (6-inch
    diameter)

Preheat oven to 350°F ✥ In a bowl combine shrimp, crab and lobster; mix well ✥ Stir in mayonnaise and chili sauce ✥ Spread evenly on tortillas, approximately 1/4" thick ✥ Place on a baking sheet and bake for 10 to 15 minutes ✥ Cut into quarters and serve.

TEMPURA SHRIMP HAND ROLL

MAKES 4 ROLLS

- 4 shrimp (21-25 count), peeled and smashed
- ½ cup flour
- 1 cup prepared tempura batter (store purchased)
- 1 qt. oil for frying

- ½ cup Sushi Rice (see recipe below)
- 2 sheets nori, cut in half
- 1 Tbsp. Masago Mayonnaise (see recipe below)

- 4 pcs. cucumber, 3" each
- 4 stalks green onion, 3" each
- ¾ cup Unagi Glaze (see recipe below)

Pinch of white sesame seeds

Coat shrimp with flour and tempura batter and fry until golden brown ❧ Flatten 2 tablespoons rice on ¾ of a sheet of nori; spread with Masago Mayonnaise; top with cucumber stick, green onion stalk and one shrimp ❧ Brush shrimp with Unagi Glaze and sprinkle with white sesame seeds ❧ Roll.

SUSHI RICE

- 4 cups cooked white rice
- ⅓ cup Sushi Su (see recipe below)

Add the Sushi Su to hot rice and mix with a wooden spoon until cool ❧ Air dry.

SUSHI SU

- ¼ cup rice vinegar
- 5 Tbsp. sugar
- 1 Tbsp. salt
- 1 pc. kombu

In a saucepan bring rice vinegar to a boil, then add the remaining ingredients and stir well until infused.

MASAGO MAYONNAISE

- 1 cup mayonnaise
- 3 Tbsp. masago
- 1 tsp. chopped garlic

Combine all ingredients; blend well.

UNAGI GLAZE

- 1 cup sugar
- 1 cup soy sauce
- 1 cup water
- 1 cup mirin
- 1 cup sake
- 1 Tbsp. dashi

In a saucepan combine all ingredients and reduce to 2 cups.

JAMES MCDONALD | I'O

THE VEGETARIAN DISH

Roasted, marinated tofu "steak" with a crown of sautéed quinoa, red lentils, Maui onions, shiitake mushrooms and crispy mixed sprout salad, served over potato purée with Carrot Ginger Sauce.

SERVES 8

24 oz. firm tofu, cut lengthwise into quarters	1 cup julienne shiitake mushrooms	4 cups potato purée or mashed potatoes
Tofu Marinade (see recipe below)	2 cups diced tomatillos	Carrot Ginger Sauce (see recipe on next page)
Vegetable spray (such as PAM)	4 cups quinoa, cooked	
Salt and pepper to taste	2 cups red lentils, cooked	4 oz. mung bean sprouts
4 Tbsp. canola oil	½ cup sake or white wine	2 oz. sunflower sprouts
2 tsp. fresh garlic, minced	4 Tbsp. chopped fresh herbs (parsley, basil, thyme, cilantro)	2 oz. radish sprouts
2 cups julienne Maui (or other sweet) onions		2 oz. your favorite light vinaigrette

Marinate tofu in Tofu Marinade at least overnight, but for no more than 24 hours ❧ Spray marinated tofu with vegetable spray and lightly season with salt and pepper ❧ Place tofu in a sauté pan over medium heat and sear on all sides ❧ Remove from pan and keep warm ❧ Return pan to heat and add canola oil and garlic ❧ Sauté garlic until lightly browned ❧ Add onions, shiitake mushrooms and tomatillos ❧ Cook until softened ❧ Add quinoa, lentils and sake and sauté until heated through ❧ Add the herbs, salt and pepper to taste and mix well ❧ Reserve warm ❧ Place ½ cup potato purée in a mound in the center of each of eight plates ❧ Top with ⅛ of the quinoa mixture ❧ Ladle some of the Carrot Ginger Sauce around each mound ❧ Cut each tofu "steak" into quarters and arrange around the mound ❧ Mix the sprouts with the vinaigrette and season with salt and pepper ❧ Divide the sprout mixture into eight equal portions and top each mound with one portion of the sprouts ❧ Serve immediately.

TOFU MARINADE

2 cups Indonesian sweet soy sauce (or substitute low salt soy sauce and honey)	2 tsp. sambal chili sauce
	2 tsp. sesame oil

Combine all ingredients; blend well ❧ Set aside and chill.

(Recipe continues on following page)

JAMES MCDONALD | I'O

CARROT GINGER SAUCE

1	lb. carrots, peeled and roughly chopped	1	bay leaf	3	Tbsp. honey
½	oz. fresh ginger, roughly chopped	1	Tbsp. minced lemongrass	½	tsp. powdered ginger
		1	cup orange juice	2	Tbsp. cornstarch, mixed with 2 tablespoons water
		1	cup ginger ale		
1	small fresh chili pepper	1	cup water		Salt to taste

In a food processor purée carrots, ginger, chili, bay leaf and lemongrass. Add orange juice, ginger ale, water, honey and powdered ginger and place in a saucepan over medium heat. Simmer for 35 minutes, then add cornstarch mixture. Simmer for two minutes more, skimming the surface of any foam. Season with salt and strain.

Chilled Hearts of Palm

ISLAND CIOPPINO

SERVES 4

2	oz. olive oil
8	scallops
4	moi filets or any firm white fish (4 oz. each)
8	mussels
8	clams
8	oz. white wine

Cioppino Sauce (see recipe below)

8	Kaua'i shrimp, peeled and deveined
4	Kaua'i shrimp, head on

In a large sauté pan over high heat, add olive oil and sear scallops for 1 minute ❧ Add fish and sauté for another minute, then add mussels and clams ❧ Deglaze with the white wine and stir in Cioppino Sauce and Kaua'i shrimp ❧ Bring to a simmer ❧ Cook for approximately 2 minutes or until the shellfish open and the seafood is just cooked through ❧ Enjoy!

CIOPPINO SAUCE

2½	oz. olive oil	½	tsp. dried oregano	1½	lbs. tomatoes, whole, peeled, in juice (crush by hand, reserve juice)
5	oz. Maui onion, julienne	½	tsp. crushed red peppers		
5	oz. red bell peppers, julienne	1½	cups fish stock or clam juice	1	tsp. chopped Italian parsley
2	oz. celery, julienne	1½	cups white wine	¼	tsp. salt
1	Tbsp. minced garlic			¼	tsp. pepper

In a sauce pot heat olive oil over medium heat ❧ Add Maui onion, bell peppers and celery ❧ Sauté for about 3 minutes to sweat the vegetables ❧ Stir in garlic, oregano and crushed red peppers; sauté for about 2 minutes, being careful not to burn the garlic ❧ Add fish stock, white wine, tomatoes and Italian parsley; simmer for about 10 minutes ❧ Season with salt and pepper ❧ Reserve ❧ Can be made a day ahead and chilled until needed.

ALAN TSUCHIYAMA | SHERATON WAIKĪKĪ

KAMUELA TOMATO & MAUI ONION GAZPACHO

YIELDS 14 CUPS

1   can (48 oz.) V-8 juice
1½ cups chopped Maui onions
1½ cups peeled, seeded and
      chopped cucumber

3   cups seeded and chopped
      Kamuela tomatoes
1½ cups chopped green bell
      peppers
½   cup chopped cilantro

1   cup extra virgin olive oil
2   Tbsp. red wine vinegar
Tabasco sauce to taste
Salt and pepper to taste
Croutons for garnish

Combine all ingredients, except croutons, in a food processor or blender; blend well. Serve chilled and garnish with croutons.

PACIFIC-STYLE BOUILLABAISSE

SERVES 5

2 oz. olive oil	10 oz. large shrimp	25 oz. Pacific-Style Bouillabaisse Stock (see recipe below)
30 oz. fresh clams, scrubbed and rinsed	17½ oz. red snapper, cubed	Salt and pepper to taste
15 oz. fresh whole mussels, cleaned	15 oz. scallops	5 oz. Red Curry Aioli (see recipe below)
	15 oz. lobster tail, quartered	10 slices toasted croutons

In a large sauté pan heat olive oil and sauté clams and mussels for 1 minute ⋅ Add shrimp, red snapper, scallops and lobster meat ⋅ Sauté until pale in color, then deglaze with the bouillabaisse stock ⋅ Simmer until the seafood is cooked, about 3 minutes ⋅ Adjust seasoning ⋅ Transfer to serving bowls ⋅ Spread the Red Curry Aioli on the toasted croutons and place on the bouillabaisse.

PACIFIC-STYLE BOUILLABAISSE STOCK

⅔ oz. olive oil	1⅜ oz. fennel, chopped	1 bay leaf
⅔ oz. butter	½ Tbsp. minced garlic	⅛ Tbsp. thyme
2¾ oz. onion, chopped	1 tsp. minced shallots	2¾ oz. white wine
⅔ oz. red bell pepper, chopped	½ Tbsp. chopped basil	22 oz. clam broth
⅔ oz. green bell pepper, chopped	½ Tbsp. chopped parsley	22 oz. shrimp stock
	Pinch of saffron	Salt and black pepper to taste

In a sauté pan heat olive oil and butter and sauté onion, bell peppers, fennel, garlic and shallots until tender ⋅ Stir in basil, parsley, saffron, bay leaf and thyme ⋅ Cook for 1 to 2 minutes ⋅ Stir in white wine, clam broth and shrimp stock ⋅ Simmer for 15 minutes ⋅ Adjust seasoning with salt and pepper and chill ⋅ Keep chilled until ready to use.

RED CURRY AIOLI

2 oz. potato, cooked	1 Tbsp. Dijon mustard	1 oz. lemon juice
2 egg yolks	1 tsp. Worcestershire sauce	2 tsp. red curry paste
3 cups olive oil	Salt and pepper to taste	2 tsp. tomato paste

Combine all ingredients and blend well.

ROY YAMAGUCHI | ROY'S RESTAURANT

THAI HOT AND SOUR MISO SOUP

With Shrimp Dumplings

SERVES 4

12 Shrimp Dumplings
     (see recipe on next page)
6   cups Chicken Stock
     (see recipe on next page)
¼   cup red miso
4   oz. enoki mushrooms
1   leek, julienne, white part
     only
½   tsp. minced ginger
½   tsp. minced garlic
3   kaffir lime leaves
2   tsp. finely minced
     lemongrass
½   tsp. rayu (spicy sesame
     oil)
1   tsp. fish sauce

⅛   tsp. shichimi
Juice of 1 lime

Garnish:
2   Tbsp. diced red
     bell pepper
2   Tbsp. diced
     yellow bell
     pepper
3   Tbsp. fresh
     cilantro
4   stalks lemongrass
     (optional)
1   tsp. furikake
     (optional)

Prepare the Shrimp Dumplings; cook and set aside. In a large stockpot combine chicken stock, miso, enoki mushrooms, leek, ginger, garlic, kaffir lime leaves, lemongrass, Rayu and fish sauce. Bring to a boil, then reduce heat and simmer for 15 minutes. Add the shichimi and lime juice, then strain into soup bowls. To serve, add 3 Shrimp Dumplings to each bowl. Sprinkle bell peppers around the edge of the soup bowl and place cilantro in the center. If desired, also garnish with the shrimp heads from the dumpling recipe and a stalk of lemongrass. Sprinkle furikake around the edge.

Lois Ellen Frank

Thai cuisine has a long tradition of hot and sour soups. Sometimes, I enjoy a bowl at my favorite Thai restaurant after a busy evening in the kitchen. Here, I combine those flavors with Japanese miso.

ROY YAMAGUCHI | ROY'S RESTAURANT

SHRIMP DUMPLINGS

1	lb. medium shrimp, peeled and deveined (reserve 8 heads for garnish, if desired)	½	tsp. minced ginger		Salt and freshly ground pepper to taste
2	Tbsp. heavy cream	⅛	tsp. minced garlic	1½	Tbsp. cornstarch
1	small egg	½	Tbsp. fish sauce	¼	cup water
		¼	cup diced water chestnuts	12	wonton wrappers
		¼	tsp. minced fresh basil		

In a food processor or blender purée shrimp, heavy cream, egg, ginger, garlic, fish sauce, water chestnuts and basil. Transfer to a bowl and season with salt and pepper. Cover with plastic wrap and refrigerate for 1 hour. In a small bowl combine cornstarch and water. Lay the wrappers on a work surface and place ½ tablespoon of the filling in the center of each. Brush the edges of the wrapper with the cornstarch mixture, gather the edges together, and twist to close. Place the dumplings on a baking sheet lined with parchment paper, cover with plastic wrap, and refrigerate for 1 hour. (The dumplings can be stored in the refrigerator for up to 2 days.) Just before service, bring a large saucepan of water to a boil and cook the dumplings for about 5 minutes or until they float to the surface.

CHICKEN STOCK

YIELDS ABOUT 1 QUART

1-2	chicken carcasses, broken up	½	cup coarsely chopped carrot	5	black peppercorns
2	Tbsp. olive oil	4	qt. water	2	bay leaves
1	stalk celery, coarsely chopped	¼	cup fresh basil leaves		Salt and freshly ground pepper to taste
½	cup coarsely chopped onion	¼	cup fresh thyme leaves		

Preheat the oven to 350°F. Place the chicken bones in a roasting pan and sprinkle with 1½ tablespoons of the oil. Roast in the oven until brown, about 15 to 20 minutes. In a large stockpot heat the remaining ½ tablespoon of the olive oil and sauté celery, onion and carrot over medium-high heat until tender. Add water, basil, thyme, peppercorns, bay leaves and roasted bones. Bring to a boil, then reduce heat and simmer until reduced by three-quarters (to about 1 quart), about 45 minutes. Periodically skim the surface of the stock to remove any impurities. Strain, discarding the solids, and season with salt and pepper.

Chef's Suggestion: For a variation use duck stock. Follow the recipe for Chicken Stock, substituting 1 to 2 duck carcasses for the chicken carcasses.

EDWIN GOTO | THE MANELE BAY HOTEL

CHILLED HEARTS OF PALM

With Asparagus and Coconut Lime Dressing

SERVES 5

20 asparagus spears, peeled, blanched and chilled

1 lb. hearts of palm, thinly sliced

1 Japanese cucumber, thinly sliced

½ lb. mixed baby greens

Coconut Lime Dressing

¼ cup roasted and chopped macadamia nuts

In a large bowl combine asparagus, hearts of palm, cucumber and mixed baby greens. Toss gently with Coconut Lime Dressing. Arrange salad on plates, sprinkle with macadamia nuts, and serve immediately.

COCONUT LIME DRESSING

½ cup coconut milk

¼ cup rice wine vinegar

⅛ cup lime juice

3 Tbsp. honey

1 cup canola oil

Kosher salt to taste

Black pepper, freshly ground to taste

In a medium-sized bowl combine coconut milk, rice wine vinegar, lime juice and honey. Stir the ingredients using a wire whisk. While constantly whisking, slowly add canola oil in a steady stream. Once all the oil is incorporated, season to taste with kosher salt and pepper. Set aside.

Castle & Cooke Resorts, LLC

CHINESE BARBEQUED DUCK SALAD

With Lilikoʻi Vinaigrette

SERVES 4

4½-5 lb. duckling
1½ cups water
⅛ cup white vinegar
3 slices ginger root
¼ bunch green onions
¼ bunch Chinese parsley

2 Tbsp. soy sauce
½ cup water
¼ tsp. five-spice powder
Lilikoʻi Vinaigrette (see recipe below)

6 oz. mesclun greens (1½ oz. per person)
Carrot strings and green onion slices for garnish

Prepare duck for hanging. Bring one cup of the water to a boil and add vinegar. Baste duck with boiling water mixture for about 2 to 3 minutes or until skin of the duck feels tight. In a stainless steel bowl mash together ginger, green onions and Chinese parsley. Add soy sauce, the remaining ½ cup of water and five-spice powder. Rub duck inside and out with this mixture. Hang duck in a cool area until skin is dry (about 7 to 8 hours). Baste well with part of the Lilikoʻi Vinaigrette. Roast duck in an oven preheated to 325°F for about 1 hour. Remove duck from oven; cool and thinly slice. In a serving bowl combine mesclun greens and Lilikoʻi Vinaigrette. Toss well and garnish with sliced duck, carrot strings and green onions.

LILIKOʻI VINAIGRETTE

Juice and zest of ½ lime
1 Tbsp. sugar
½ tsp. black pepper
1 clove garlic
½ tsp. chopped ginger
1 cup rice vinegar
¼ cup lilikoʻi (passion fruit) purée, unsweetened
3 cups salad oil
¼ cup honey

Combine all ingredients in a food processor or blender and blend until smooth.

Ric Noyle

DAVID BOUCHER | HYATT REGENCY KAUA'I

GRILLED KAUA'I SWEET ONIONS AND VINE-RIPENED TOMATOES

SERVES 1

4	slices local sweet onions	1	tsp. minced ginger		Black Pepper Lychee Vinaigrette	
½	cup mirin		Marinated Tomatoes (see		(see recipe below)	
1	Tbsp. brown sugar		recipe below)			

Slice onions thinly ✍ Blend together remaining ingredients and pour over onions to marinate ✍ Grill onions until soft ✍ Serve at room temperature ✍ Arrange on plate artfully with Marinated Tomatoes and dress with Black Pepper Lychee Vinaigrette.

MARINATED TOMATOES

4	slices vine-ripened tomatoes	2	tsp. chopped basil
2	tsp. minced garlic	2	Tbsp. olive oil
1	tsp. minced ginger		

Cut tomatoes into ¼"-thick slices ✍ Blend together remaining ingredients and pour over tomatoes to marinate.

BLACK PEPPER LYCHEE VINAIGRETTE

4	oz. balsamic vinegar	20	oz. lychee (canned or
2	oz. rice wine vinegar		fresh, peeled and pitted)
2	oz. black pepper, freshly ground	5	oz. olive oil
2	oz. sugar		Kosher salt to taste
2	oz. water		

In a saucepan combine balsamic vinegar, rice wine vinegar and pepper ✍ Bring to a boil and reduce by one-half ✍ In another saucepan bring sugar and water to a boil ✍ Puree lychee in their juice and add to simple syrup ✍ Combine pepper mixture and lychee mixture ✍ Add oil and adjust seasoning to taste.

Dana Edmunds

KATAIFI AND MACADAMIA NUT-CRUSTED BLACK TIGER PRAWNS

With Big Island Baby Greens and Pineapple Vinaigrette

SERVES 4

8 jumbo black tiger prawns, peeled
¼ Tbsp. lemon juice
Salt and pepper to taste
8 bamboo sticks
2 Tbsp. all-purpose flour
1 Tbsp. cornstarch

1 Tbsp. chopped macadamia nuts
1 egg, lightly beaten
4 Tbsp. cold water
1 box kataifi (shredded filo dough) or any thin noodles

4 cups vegetable oil for deep-frying
Big Island baby greens
Pineapple Vinaigrette (see recipe below)

Marinate prawns with lemon juice, salt and pepper The acid from the lemon juice will make the meat of the shrimp crunchy Skewer each prawn with a bamboo stick; set aside In a mixing bowl combine flour, cornstarch, macadamia nuts, egg and cold water; blend well Dip each prawn in the batter, then wrap with the kataifi Repeat with all the prawns In a wok or deep fryer heat the oil to about 375°F, then fry the prawns for a few minutes or until golden brown Serve on Big Island baby greens and drizzle with Pineapple Vinaigrette.

PINEAPPLE VINAIGRETTE

½ cup pineapple juice
1 Tbsp. sugar
1 Tbsp. white vinegar

Pinch of salt
Dash of Tabasco sauce

In a saucepan combine all the ingredients and bring to a boil Reduce heat and simmer for a few minutes Serve at room temperature.

Kyle Rothenborg

PHILIPPE PADOVANI | PADOVANI'S RESTAURANT & WINE BAR

SAUTÉED SCALLOPS

With Hearts of Palm and Prosciutto Salad

SERVES 4

2   Tbsp. olive oil
16   fresh scallops (8 count)
Hearts of Palm and Prosciutto Salad
      (see recipe below)
½   cup julienne mango

Heat a Teflon® pan and add olive oil ❧ Sauté scallops until golden brown ❧ Set aside ❧ Take four chilled 12" plates ❧ In the center of each plate, place the hearts of palm salad in equal amounts and surround the salad with cooked scallops ❧ Sprinkle with mango ❧ Serve immediately.

HEARTS OF PALM AND PROSCIUTTO SALAD

1   Tbsp. sherry vinegar
4   Tbsp. olive oil
Salt and pepper to taste
4   cups julienne hearts of palm
¼   cup finely diced prosciutto
1   Tbsp. finely chopped chives

In a screw-top jar combine sherry vinegar, olive oil, salt and pepper ❧ Cover tightly and shake vigorously for 20 seconds ❧ In a mixing bowl combine hearts of palm, prosciutto and chives with the vinaigrette, then season to taste ❧ Set aside.

Franzen Photography

71

SMOKED DUCK SALAD

With Pear, Gorgonzola, Walnut and Fennel Orange Citronette

SERVES 4

1	cup fresh orange juice
1	Tbsp. fennel seed, crushed
½	vanilla bean, cut open and scraped
2	tsp. sherry vinegar
⅛	tsp. ground cinnamon

1	Tbsp. hot water
16	oz. boneless duck breast, lightly smoked
8	oz. baby lettuce leaves, rinsed and drained

8	oz. gorgonzola cheese, crumbled
4	oz. walnut halves, lightly roasted
1	ripe pear

Preheat oven to 350°F. In a mixing bowl combine orange juice, fennel seeds, vanilla, sherry vinegar, cinnamon and hot water; mix well. Refrigerate until ready to use. Prepare the duck breast by smoking over hardwood for approximately 10 minutes and then placing onto a baking sheet. Place the duck, skin up, into preheated oven and roast until done. In a mixing bowl toss lettuce leaves with enough dressing to lightly coat the lettuce. Divide the lettuce among four large salad plates. Thinly slice duck breasts and fan them onto each plate. Sprinkle lettuce with gorgonzola cheese and walnuts and then drizzle the remaining dressing over the four salads. Cut the pear into four quarters and slice thinly. Place one pear fan on each salad and serve.

Chef's Suggestion: Use apple wood chips for smoking the duck.

SPICY CRAB AND SHRIMP NAPOLEON

SERVES 4

12 wonton skins	2 Tbsp. chopped scallions	8 shiso leaves
Peanut oil for frying	2 tsp. sambal olek	1 bunch radish sprouts
6 oz. cooked shrimp, chopped	2 tsp. tobiko caviar	½ cup pickled ginger
6 oz. cooked crabmeat, flaked	Presentation:	1 Tbsp. tobiko caviar
2 Tbsp. mayonnaise	Green Papaya Salad (see recipe below)	

Fry wonton skins in peanut oil until crisp and golden brown. In a bowl combine shrimp and half each of the mayonnaise, scallions, sambal olek and tobiko caviar; toss lightly to mix. In another bowl combine crab and the remaining half of the mayonnaise, scallions, sambal olek and tobiko caviar; toss lightly to mix. Place a wonton on a plate and top with one-fourth of the shrimp mixture, then top with another wonton. Place a shiso leaf on the wonton and spoon on one tablespoon Green Papaya Salad. Top with another wonton, one-fourth of the crab mixture and a shiso leaf. Garnish with radish sprouts. Divide remaining Green Papaya Salad between the four plates. Garnish with pickled ginger and tobiko caviar.

GREEN PAPAYA SALAD

1 cup shredded green papaya	¼ cup bottled sweet Thai chili sauce	2 Tbsp. julienne red onion
⅓ cup shredded carrot		1 Tbsp. chopped cilantro
¼ cup lime juice	¼ cup julienne red bell pepper	1 Tbsp. toasted sesame seeds

In a bowl combine all ingredients and toss lightly to mix.

DAVID PAUL JOHNSON | DAVID PAUL'S LAHAINA GRILL

TOY BOX TOMATO SALAD

SERVES 4

2	cups chopped tiger tomatoes
⅓	cup apple juice
2	shallots, chopped
⅓	cup rice wine vinegar
½	cup basil, loosely packed

Salt and pepper to taste
2   Tbsp. extra virgin olive oil
¾   cup sweet 100s red tomatoes
¾   cup red pear tomatoes
¾   cup sweet 100s yellow tomatoes

¾   cup yellow pear tomatoes
¾   cup red currant tomatoes
4   sprigs basil
2   Tbsp. Maui onion, finely diced
Freshly ground black pepper

In a blender combine tiger tomatoes, apple juice, shallots, rice wine vinegar, basil, salt, pepper and olive oil; blend well. Strain and chill. Clean and stem all the baby tomatoes; slice some in half. Divide tomatoes among four martini glasses and pour sauce over the tomatoes up to the halfway point. Garnish with a sprig of basil, chopped onion and black pepper.

EDWIN GOTO | THE MANELE BAY HOTEL

WARM CALAMARI

With Spiced Cabbage Slaw and Pineapple Dressing

SERVES 5

½   cup cornstarch
⅛   cup all-purpose flour
1   qt. canola oil
1   lb. calamari, cleaned, cut into
    rings and dried of excess
    moisture

Spiced Cabbage Slaw
    (see recipe below)
Pineapple Dressing
    (see recipe below)

Castle & Cooke Resorts, LLC

Combine cornstarch and flour on a plate. Select a medium-sized pot with a thick bottom. Add canola oil and place over medium-high heat to warm the oil. When the oil is ready, toss calamari with the cornstarch-flour mixture, coating lightly and evenly. Gently place calamari into hot oil and fry until crispy, about 1 minute. Remove calamari and place onto paper towels to remove excess oil. Toss calamari with cabbage slaw and serve immediately.

SPICED CABBAGE SLAW

2   cups green cabbage, thinly sliced
2   cups red cabbage, thinly sliced
¼   cup mint leaves, chopped
¼   cup thinly sliced green onions

3   radishes, thinly sliced
Pineapple Dressing (see recipe
    below)

Kosher salt to taste
Freshly ground black pepper
    to taste

In a mixing bowl combine cabbage, mint, green onions and radishes; mix well. Add Pineapple Dressing and toss to mix. Season with salt and pepper.

PINEAPPLE DRESSING

2   Tbsp. tamarind paste
1   tsp. Thai curry paste
¼   cup pineapple juice

½   cup honey
1   cup canola oil
2   tsp. kosher salt

¼   tsp. freshly ground black
    pepper

In a small saucepan combine tamarind paste, curry paste and pineapple juice and cook over low heat. Simmer until tamarind has dissolved, then stir in honey. Remove from heat and slowly whisk in canola oil and season with salt and pepper.

Chef Sam's Oriental Lamb Chops with Rotelli Pasta

ASIAN-STYLE OSSO BUCCO

SERVES 4

¼   cup all-purpose flour
4   osso bucco (veal shanks),
      2" diameter
2   Tbsp. peanut oil
¼   cup white wine
3   cups veal stock
1½-inch pc. ginger root,
      peeled and sliced
1   star anise
½   cup diced tomatoes
½   cup sliced fresh shiitake
      mushrooms
1   Tbsp. soy sauce
1   tsp. orange zest
1   Tbsp. lemon juice
2   Tbsp. cornstarch
¼   cup water
Salt and black pepper to taste

Ric Noyle

Lightly flour veal shanks on both sides ❧ Heat a braising pan and add peanut oil ❧ Sauté veal shanks until golden brown on all sides ❧ Add white wine, veal stock, ginger, star anise, tomatoes, shiitake mushrooms, soy sauce, orange zest and lemon juice ❧ Bring to a boil and cover ❧ Place in oven preheated to 350°F and let it braise for about 2 hours ❧ (Check veal after 1½ hours as some ovens run a little hot ❧ The meat should be soft to the touch and slightly fall away from the bone.) ❧ When veal is done, remove from the pan and set aside in a warm place ❧ Mix together cornstarch and water to make a smooth paste and add to the boiling stock ❧ Let simmer for about 4 minutes ❧ Season with salt and black pepper ❧ Strain and ladle sauce over veal shank before service.

BRAISED SHORT RIBS

With Creamy Herb Polenta and Cabernet Thyme Reduction

SERVES 10

10 portions short ribs	2 oz. tomato paste	½ oz. thyme sprigs
Vegetable oil as needed	8 oz. cabernet red wine	Salt and pepper to taste
3 oz. carrots, diced	16 oz. brown stock	Creamy Herb Polenta (see recipe
3 oz. onions, diced	24 oz. brown sauce	below)
3 oz. celery, diced	2 bay leaves	

In a sauce pot heat vegetable oil and brown short ribs on both sides ‰ Remove the short ribs and set aside ‰ Stir in carrots, onions and celery and cook until caramelized ‰ Add tomato paste; stir and let cook for 1 minute ‰ Add red wine and reduce by half ‰ Add brown stock, brown sauce, bay leaves and thyme and bring to a simmer ‰ Return short ribs to sauce pot, cover, and braise in the oven at 350°F until fork tender ‰ Remove ribs; degrease sauce, strain, and adjust taste with salt and pepper ‰ Serve ribs with polenta and lace with sauce.

CREAMY HERB POLENTA

1 oz. shallots, finely diced	1 qt. light cream	2 Tbsp. chopped chervil
2 Tbsp. finely diced garlic	1 lb. yellow cornmeal	1 Tbsp. chopped oregano
2 oz. butter	4 oz. grated Parmesan cheese	Salt and pepper to taste
1½ qt. chicken stock	¼ cup basil, chopped	

In a saucepan sauté shallots and garlic in butter until they are translucent ‰ Add chicken stock and cream and bring to a boil ‰ Add cornmeal in a steady stream, stirring constantly, until it has been all added ‰ Simmer the mixture for 30 minutes ‰ Remove the pot from the heat and blend in Parmesan cheese and herbs ‰ Season with salt and pepper.

CHARCOALED FLANK STEAK

With Roasted Moloka'i Sweet Potatoes, Maui Onions, Tomatoes and Chimichurri Sauce

SERVES 5

2 lbs. flank steak	3 tomatoes, core removed and cut into wedges	Orange Dressing (see recipe below)
3 Tbsp. olive oil	1 medium Maui onion, peeled and thinly sliced	2 lbs. Moloka'i sweet potatoes, cut into wedges and roasted
3 Tbsp. ancho chili powder or to taste	3-4 heads frisee lettuce, picked and washed	Chimichurri Sauce (see recipe below)
Kosher salt and freshly ground pepper to taste		

Coat the flank steak with olive oil and season with ancho chili powder, salt and pepper. Place on the hottest section of the grill and cook for about 4 minutes on each side. While the steak is cooking prepare the salad. Combine tomatoes, Maui onion and lettuce in a large mixing bowl and season with salt and pepper. Add Orange Dressing and gently toss. Arrange salad on plates and add sweet potato wedges. Once steak is done, allow it to rest for 5 minutes. Place steak onto cutting board and carve against the grain with a sharp knife. Arrange steak on salad and drizzle with Chimichurri Sauce. Serve immediately.

ORANGE DRESSING

1 cup fresh orange juice	Kosher salt to taste	1 Tbsp. honey
4 oz. rice wine vinegar	1 Tbsp. freshly ground black pepper	
10 oz. olive oil		

In a blender combine all of the ingredients and purée.

CHIMICHURRI SAUCE

1 cup olive oil	10 cloves garlic, medium size	½ tsp. cayenne pepper
½ cup cider vinegar	2 tsp. freshly ground black pepper	½ Tbsp. kosher salt
1 cup fresh parsley		
¼ cup fresh oregano		

In a blender combine all of the ingredients and purée. Taste and adjust seasoning. Reserve for further use.

CHEF SAM'S ORIENTAL LAMB CHOPS

With Rotelli Pasta

SERVES 4-6

Doug Peebles

Marinade (see recipe below)
2-3 lamb chops per serving (8 to 18 chops total)
2　Tbsp. butter
4　Tbsp. olive oil
1½ Tbsp. minced garlic
1　medium carrot, julienne
2　medium zucchini, julienne
2　cups julienne shiitake mushrooms

½　cup coarsely chopped Chinese parsley
12　oz. rotelli, cooked according to package directions, drained
1½ cups heavy cream
Salt and pepper to taste
¾　cup grated Parmesan cheese
Fresh basil sprigs for garnish

Massage marinade into lamb chops, then let marinate 4 to 6 hours in the refrigerator. In a large saucepan heat butter and olive oil over medium-high heat. Cook garlic for about 1 minute, without browning, then add vegetables and stir-fry for 2 to 3 minutes. Add drained, cooked rotelli and stir-fry another minute. Add heavy cream, bring to a boil, then immediately reduce to a simmer. Adjust seasoning with salt and pepper. Just before serving, fold in Parmesan cheese and let cook 1 minute. Broil lamb to perfection (about 2 to 3 minutes per side for medium-rare or to your liking). Serve rotelli in large pasta bowls with 2 or 3 Oriental lamb chops on top; garnish with sprigs of fresh basil.

MARINADE

½　cup soy sauce
¾　cup minced garlic
1　Tbsp. minced fresh ginger

2　cups brown sugar
½　tsp. chili flakes
½　cup minced basil

½　cup minced Chinese parsley
Salt to taste

Combine all ingredients; blend well.

GRILLED COLORADO LAMB

With Baby Vegetables, Yukon Gold Mashed Potatoes and Smoked Tomato Demi-Glace

SERVES 2

1 rack large Colorado lamb, Frenched	3 oz. unsalted butter, room temperature	2 baby carrots, blanched
Salt and pepper to taste	Salt and pepper to taste	6 French green beans, blanched
¾ lb. Yukon gold potatoes, peeled	3 oz. milk, scalded	4 oz. Tomato Demi-Glace (see recipe below)
	4 stalks asparagus, blanched	Chopped parsley for garnish

Cut lamb rack into four double-bone lamb chops and season with salt and pepper. Keep refrigerated while grill heats up. Cut potatoes into eighths and boil in salted water until soft. Place into a large mixing bowl and whisk in butter, salt, pepper and milk. Cover tightly and let stand in a warm place until ready to serve. Grill lamb to your liking, while you lightly sauté the vegetables in a little bit of unsalted butter. When ready to assemble the entrées, place a mound of mashed potatoes in the middle of the plate and place two of the four chops leaning up on the potatoes, bones pointing up into the air. Place half of the vegetables on the opposite side of the plate from the lamb. Drape the Tomato Demi-Glace over the lamb chops and onto the plate. Garnish the sauce with the fine dice of smoked tomato and chopped parsley.

TOMATO DEMI-GLACE

There are very few products available to the home cook to properly produce demi-glace so I am recommending that you go to a restaurant that makes demi-glace. Purchase 4 to 6 ounces and season it yourself with smoked tomatoes. To do this, one would place tomatoes, which have been cut in half, into a smoker with thick hardwood smoke for approximately 5 minutes. Place one half of a tomato into a sauce pot with the demi-glace, bring to just before boiling, and simmer for 5 minutes. Taste and adjust seasonings. Strain the sauce and keep warm. Peel and seed the rest of the smoked tomato and dice fine for garnish.

Chef's Suggestion: A nice full-bodied zinfandel or medium-bodied cabernet will go wonderfully with this dish.

COREY WAITE | HAPUNA BEACH PRINCE HOTEL

GRILLED SZECHWAN RACK OF LAMB

With Peppercorn Crust and Star Anise Sauce

SERVES 4

1	Lamb Glaze (see recipe below)	1	star anise	1	tsp. red peppercorn
1	shallot, minced	2	cups red wine	1	tsp. white peppercorn
½	bay leaf	1	cup lamb stock (or beef if you	1	tsp. black peppercorn
1	Tbsp. olive oil		can not get lamb bones)	2	racks of lamb (about 1 lb.
4	cracked black peppercorns		Salt and pepper to taste		each)

Prepare the Lamb Glaze. In a medium saucepan sweat the shallot and bay leaf in olive oil. Add cracked black peppercorns and star anise. Stir in the red wine and reduce by ¾. When the sauce has reached the proper consistency, add the stock and reduce by half. Season to taste with salt and pepper. Using a small sauté pan or a pepper grinder, roughly crack the three different peppercorns and put into a small bowl. With a small brush, glaze the racks with the Lamb Glaze. Lightly coat the lamb rack with the trio of peppercorns and grill to desired doneness.

LAMB GLAZE

½ cup barbecue sauce
   (i.e., Bull's Eye)
¼ cup hoisin sauce
3 Tbsp. Thai chili sauce
2 Tbsp. honey
2 Tbsp. cider vinegar
Salt and pepper to taste

In a medium saucepan combine all ingredients, except salt and pepper, and cook until thickened. Season to taste with salt and pepper.

ALAN TSUCHIYAMA | SHERATON WAIKĪKĪ

HOISIN HONEY-GLAZED LAMB CHOPS

With Wasabi Garlic Mashed Potatoes

SERVES 8

1 cup hoisin sauce	2 Tbsp. white sesame seeds, toasted	16 double lamb chops, trimmed
¼ cup honey	2 Tbsp. black sesame seeds	Salt and pepper to taste
2 Tbsp. soy sauce	2 Tbsp. salad oil	Wasabi Garlic Mashed Potatoes (see
2 Tbsp. finely chopped green onions	Togarashi (Japanese chili pepper) to taste	recipe below)

Combine hoisin sauce, honey, soy sauce, green onions, sesame seeds, salad oil and togarashi; blend well. Lightly season lamb chops with salt and pepper. Broil lamb chops, basting with the glaze. Place Wasabi Garlic Mashed Potatoes in center of plate and place two double chops next to potatoes with the bones crossed.

WASABI GARLIC MASHED POTATOES

2 lbs. russet potatoes, peeled, cut into 1-inch cubes and steamed	1 cup heavy whipping cream, hot	4 tsp. wasabi paste
	3 Tbsp. unsalted butter	Salt and white pepper to taste
	2 tsp. finely chopped garlic	

In large mixing bowl whip together all ingredients while still hot.

PEPPER-COATED LĀNA'I VENISON LOIN

With Pohā Berry Essence and Poppy Seed Spatzle

SERVES 8

2   cups red wine
1   Tbsp. crushed juniper berries
1   cup fresh pohā berries or pohā
      berry chutney
3   cups venison demi-glace
      (prepare with bones)
4   oz. soft butter

4   lbs. venison loin, bone in
      (4 oz. boneless tenderloin
      per person)
Salt to taste
½   cup crushed colored
      peppercorns

4   oz. macadamia nut oil
Poppy Seed Spatzle (see recipe
      below)
Stir-fry vegetables in season
Whole pohā berries, if available

In a stockpot combine red wine, juniper berries and pohā berries; blend well. Add demi-glace and bring to a boil, then reduce heat and simmer for 40 minutes. Strain and blend in soft butter. Cut venison loin into 4-ounce steaks or leave loin whole; season with salt and coat with peppercorns. Sear in a hot pan with macadamia nut oil on all sides to desired doneness. Slice half of the steak at an angle and cut 2 medallions per serving. Arrange on plate with sautéed Poppy Seed Spatzle. Decorate with stir-fry vegetables and whole pohā berries. Ladle sauce around the meat.

POPPY SEED SPATZLE

1   lb. flour
7   eggs
Salt, pepper and nutmeg to taste

¼   cup poppy seeds
1   gallon salted water

1   cup vegetable oil
2   Tbsp. butter

In a bowl combine flour, eggs, salt, pepper, nutmeg and poppy seeds. Blend to a smooth paste and beat with the palm of your hand until air bubbles appear. In a stockpot bring salted water and vegetable oil to a boil. Fill spatzle press with flour mixture and press into boiling water. When spatzle floats to the top, remove and cool off in ice water. Drain and reserve. Sauté in butter until golden brown.

Chef's Suggestion: Venison could be substituted with Parker Ranch beef tenderloin.

SMOKED KĀLUA PORK

With Savoy Cabbage and Ponzu Shiitake Sauce

SERVES 10

3 lbs. pork butt	2 ti leaves	Liquid smoke to taste
4 oz. Hawaiian salt	1 large Savoy cabbage	6 oz. fresh poi
Crushed black pepper to taste	1 large Maui onion	Ponzu Shiitake Sauce (see recipe
1 quart water	2 Tbsp. butter	below)

Preheat oven to 375°F. Season pork butt with Hawaiian salt and black pepper. Roast in oven for 1 hour. Remove meat and deglaze roasting pan with water. Boil on stove until all the drippings are melted. Cut pork butt into 1" cubes and place in stockpot. Add liquid from roasting pan and additional water, until pork is barely covered. Top with ti leaves. Cover the pot with a lid and cook until pork is soft and can be shredded with a fork. Remove all the leaves from the Savoy cabbage, reserving the heart and small yellow leaves. Quickly blanch leaves in boiling salted water for 2 minutes and cool off in ice water. Chop Maui onion, cabbage heart and small yellow leaves into small pieces. Sauté in butter. Add shredded kālua pork and cook together until liquid is reduced. Check taste and season with liquid smoke or Hawaiian salt. Stir in poi; blend well and set aside. Trim the stems of the blanched cabbage leaves. Place a leaf in the palm of your hand and fill with 4 ounces of the kālua pig mixture. Press firmly, so cabbage leaf covers the mixture to form a tennis ball-size shape. Set on a buttered insert pan and cover with plastic wrap. Heat in oven for 7 minutes before serving.

PONZU SHIITAKE SAUCE

2 Tbsp. sesame oil	½ cup soy sauce	Juice of 1 orange
2 cups shiitake mushrooms, sliced	½ cup rice vinegar	Dash of red pepper flakes
(soaked overnight, if dried)	1 cup chicken stock	½ cup cornstarch, diluted with water
1 cup mirin	Juice of 1 lemon	4 oz. butter, softened

In a saucepan heat sesame oil and sauté shiitake mushrooms; remove and set aside. Deglaze pan with mirin, soy sauce, rice vinegar, chicken stock, lemon and orange juice. Add red pepper flakes and boil for 8 to 10 minutes. Stir in cornstarch mixture. As sauce thickens lightly, whip in the softened butter and add in the sautéed shiitake mushrooms.

Presentation: Arrange kālua pig wrapped in cabbage on soup plate and ladle 2 ounces of sauce around it.

Note: In Hawai'i, this pork is usually done in an imu pit with a whole pig wrapped in banana leaves and cooked in the ground for 6 to 8 hours.

Korean Spicy Chicken

DANIEL DELBREL | SHERATON MOANA SURFRIDER

BROILED MARINATED CHICKEN BREAST

With Tamarind Ginger Sauce, Pineapple Bell Pepper Relish and Moloka'i Sweet Potato

SERVES 6

Chicken Marinade (see recipe below)
6 chicken breasts
1½ oz. Chinese Vegetables (see recipe on next page)

2 oz. Tamarind Ginger Sauce (see recipe below)
2 oz. Pineapple Bell Pepper Relish (see recipe on next page)

3 slices (1¾ oz. each) cooked purple sweet potato*
Rosemary Salt Mix to taste (see recipe on next page)

Pour Chicken Marinade over chicken breasts and marinate in the refrigerator for at least 3 hours before cooking ♣ Season with rosemary salt and grill.

Presentation: Place Chinese Vegetables on a large serving platter; top with grilled chicken breasts ♣ Spoon over Tamarind Ginger Sauce and top each chicken breast with Pineapple Bell Pepper Relish ♣ Place the purple sweet potatoes around the chicken like a fence.

*Boil sweet potatoes whole and chill with skin on to retain a nice bright blue color.

CHICKEN MARINADE

2 oz. red wine vinegar
2 oz. lemon juice
2 oz. Kikkoman soy sauce

8 bay leaves
1 oz. crushed black peppercorn

2 oz. salad oil
2 Tbsp. patis

Combine all ingredients and blend well.

TAMARIND GINGER SAUCE

11 oz. chicken stock
2 oz. tamarind juice
1 oz. brown sugar

1½ oz. ginger, peeled and smashed
Modified food cornstarch to taste

1 Tbsp. chili paste with soya bean oil

In a saucepan bring chicken stock to a boil ♣ Add tamarind juice, brown sugar and ginger ♣ Simmer for about 5 minutes ♣ Remove ginger, then thicken with cornstarch ♣ Season with chili paste.

DANIEL DELBREL | SHERATON MOANA SURFRIDER

PINEAPPLE BELL PEPPER RELISH

12 oz. pineapple, diced
1¼ oz. green bell pepper, diced
2½ oz. red bell pepper, diced
1¼ oz. red onions, diced

Chopped cilantro to taste
Chopped scallion (green onion)
   to taste
1½ oz. olive oil

1   tsp. patis
Dash of lemon juice
Salt to taste
White pepper to taste

Combine all ingredients; mix well ᴥ Keep chilled.

CHINESE VEGETABLES

1   tsp. butter
1   tsp. chopped Maui onions or
     shallots
1½ shiitake mushrooms, cut in
     quarters and steamed or blanched

6   Chinese peas, blanched in
     salted boiling water, then
     chilled in iced water

Rosemary Salt Mix to taste
   (see recipe below)

In a sauté pan heat butter and sauté onions ᴥ Add mushrooms and Chinese peas ᴥ Season with rosemary salt.

ROSEMARY SALT MIX

4   oz. sea salt
1   oz. finely ground rosemary
1   oz. finely ground black pepper

Combine all ingredients and blend well ᴥ Keep in a dry place.

CRISPY THAI CHICKEN

With Spicy Fish Sauce

SERVES 6

¼ cup minced lemongrass	½ cup mochi rice flour	3 lbs. boneless chicken
6 cloves garlic, minced	½ cup chopped green onions	Oil for sautéing or deep-frying
1½ Tbsp. minced ginger	½ cup chopped Chinese parsley	Organic salad greens
2 Tbsp. fish sauce	2 Tbsp. cornstarch	Rice vermicelli
1 Tbsp. Hawaiian salt	2 egg whites, slightly beaten	Spicy Fish Sauce (see recipe below)

Combine lemongrass, garlic, ginger, fish sauce, Hawaiian salt, mochi rice flour, green onions, Chinese parsley, cornstarch and egg whites; blend well ❧ Add chicken and marinate overnight, if possible ❧ Sauté or deep-fry chicken until golden brown ❧ Place organic salad greens in a bowl and add chicken and rice vermicelli ❧ Drizzle with Spicy Fish Sauce and toss lightly ❧ Arrange attractively in individual bowls.

SPICY FISH SAUCE

½ cup red wine vinegar	¼ cup sugar	1 Hawaiian chili pepper, crushed and chopped
½ cup water	2 Tbsp. fish sauce	

Combine all ingredients and blend well.

KĀLUA DUCK

With Plum Wine Sauce and Lundburg Rice

SERVES 4 AS A MAIN COURSE OR 8 AS AN APPETIZER

2   ducks, boned
2   qts. duck fat, rendered, or light
     cooking oil
2   oz. liquid smoke

8   large cloves garlic, peeled
½   oz. black peppercorns
1   Tbsp. kosher salt
1   Tbsp. ground black pepper

Lundburg Rice (see recipe on
     next page)
Plum Wine Duck Sauce (see
     recipe on next page)

Divide each duck into four parts, leaving bone in leg and main wing bone on breast. Season and grill duck pieces until brown on both sides. Heat duck fat to 275°F. Put duck into an ovenproof pot and pour duck fat and liquid smoke over duck pieces until completely covered. Add garlic and peppercorns. Cover with lid or foil and bake at 350°F for 2 to 3 hours or until meat falls off the bones. Let oil and duck cool to room temperature, then drain oil and place duck and garlic in a shallow pan or ovenproof dish. To serve, reheat duck in a medium oven or in a skillet over medium heat. Place Lundburg Rice in center of plate; place duck on the rice and drizzle with Plum Wine Duck Sauce. Garnish with confit garlic saved from duck fat.

(Recipes continue on following page)

Steve Brinkman

LUNDBURG RICE

1	cup chopped onion	¼	cup Japanese plum wine	3	cups clear chicken or duck stock
½	cup finely chopped shallots	2	cups Lundburg mixed rice	½	cup finely chopped parsley
2	Tbsp. unsalted butter				

In a saucepan with a heavy bottom, sauté onions and shallots in unsalted butter over medium heat. Deglaze with plum wine. Add rice and sauté for 2 minutes. Add stock, reduce heat to a simmer, and cover pot. When all liquid is absorbed, remove rice from pan and air out before serving. Sprinkle with parsley.

PLUM WINE DUCK SAUCE

	Duck carcass, cut into 1-inch pieces	2	cups Japanese plum wine	1	Tbsp. peppercorns
3	cups diced celery, carrots, onions and leeks in equal parts	1	gallon chicken stock or water	2	shallots, finely chopped
		2	bay leaves		

In a large two-gallon stockpot, brown duck bones and parts over high heat, rendering any fat. Dispose of fat and add vegetables. Continue to brown for five minutes. Deglaze with plum wine and add stock, bay leaves, peppercorns and shallots. Bring to a boil and skim off fat and foam. Cook over low heat until reduced by half. Strain, skim fat, and continue to reduce until liquid becomes shiny and thick. When this happens, there should be about two cups of sauce to work with. This is known as a reduction sauce, which is intense and full-bodied.

DAVID BOUCHER | HYATT REGENCY KAUA'I

KOREAN SPICY CHICKEN

SERVES 4

4   chicken breasts, split into 2 pieces
½   cup milk
4   oz. flour
2   cups oil for frying
1   oz. vegetable oil
¼   tsp. minced garlic
1   head won bok, chopped
2   baby bok choy, cut in half
2   oz. mixed bell peppers, julienne

2   oz. carrots, thick julienne
4   snow pea pods, whole
½   oz. mung bean sprouts
2   oz. Korean Spicy Chicken Sauce (see recipe below)
4   scoops rice
Green onions, thinly sliced for garnish
Black sesame seeds for garnish
Carrot curls for garnish

Marinate chicken breasts in milk ⚬ Dredge chicken in flour ⚬ Preheat oil for frying to 350°F ⚬ Fry in oil for 8 minutes or until golden brown and firm ⚬ Preheat wok, add the one ounce oil and garlic, and fry until soft ⚬ Add won bok, bok choy, bell peppers, carrots, snow peas and mung bean sprouts ⚬ Continue to fry until hot, but still crisp ⚬ Add fried chicken and Korean Spicy Chicken Sauce and toss to coat well ⚬ Arrange chicken breasts, rice and vegetables on plate ⚬ Garnish with green onions, black sesame seeds and carrot curls ⚬ Enjoy!

KOREAN SPICY CHICKEN SAUCE

½   oz. chopped garlic
¾   tsp. sesame oil
2   cups soy sauce
2   cups sugar

¾   Tbsp. sambal olek
¾   tsp. chili powder
½   oz. green onion, chopped
12   oz. water

¾   tsp. crushed red pepper
1   oz. honey
½   oz. cornstarch slurry, as needed

In a saucepan lightly sauté garlic in sesame oil; then add soy sauce, sugar, sambal olek, chili powder, green onion, water, red pepper and honey; bring to a boil ⚬ Thicken with cornstarch slurry to obtain a maple syrup consistency.

MACADAMIA NUT CHICKEN BREASTS

With Tropical Marmalade

SERVES 6

6 chicken breast halves, boneless and skinless
Chicken Barbeque Marinade (see recipe below)
1 cup finely chopped macadamia nuts

¾ cup fine dry bread crumbs
½ cup all-purpose flour
3 eggs, lightly beaten
2 Tbsp. oil

1 Tbsp. butter
Tropical Marmalade (see recipe below)

Marinate chicken in Chicken Barbeque Marinade for 1 hour, turning occasionally ❧ Remove the chicken and allow to drain ❧ Combine macadamia nuts and bread crumbs ❧ Dredge chicken in flour, dip in beaten eggs, and coat with the macadamia nut mixture ❧ In a heavy skillet heat oil and butter over medium heat ❧ Sauté chicken for 6 to 8 minutes, turning once ❧ Add a little more oil if necessary, since macadamia nuts may absorb oil ❧ Serve with Tropical Marmalade.

CHICKEN BARBEQUE MARINADE

½ cup soy sauce
1½ Tbsp. brown sugar

1 Tbsp. mirin (Japanese sweet rice wine)
1 Tbsp. olive oil

1 tsp. minced fresh garlic
1 tsp. minced fresh ginger

Combine all ingredients; blend well.

TROPICAL MARMALADE

2 cups diced fresh pineapple
3 cups diced fresh papaya
½ cup fresh cape gooseberries (pohā berries), optional

6 Tbsp. granulated sugar or to taste
⅛ tsp. prepared horseradish, optional

⅛ tsp. chopped fresh mint or spearmint, optional

In a saucepan combine all ingredients, except mint ❧ Bring to a boil, then simmer for an hour or until the mixture reaches jam consistency ❧ Stir frequently to avoid scorching ❧ Cool ❧ Fold in the fresh mint to taste.

ROASTED MUSCOVY DUCK BREAST

With Pickled Ginger Plum Sauce, Moloka'i Sweet Potato Purée and Braised Endive

SERVES 4

4 Muscovy duck breasts (1 lb. each)	2 plums, cut into halves, then cut into fans	Braised Endive (see recipe on next page)
Salt and white pepper to taste	Sweet Potato Purée (see recipe below)	Pickled Ginger Plum Sauce (see recipe on page 97)
1 Tbsp. butter		

Generously salt fatty side of duck breasts ❧ Cook them, fat side down, in a heavy frying pan over low heat for 12 minutes ❧ Three quarters of the way through the cooking turn the duck breasts over to sear the other side ❧ Remove the breasts, set aside, and keep warm ❧ In a frying pan heat butter and sauté the plums for a few minutes until cooked ❧ Set aside for garnish ❧ Preheat four dinner plates ❧ Spoon one quenelle of the Sweet Potato Purée on each plate ❧ Place an endive half on the plate next to the purée ❧ Pour 2 ounces of Pickled Ginger Plum Sauce onto plate, avoiding the purée and endive ❧ Slice duck breast into eight slices and arrange over the sauce ❧ Garnish with plum fan ❧ Serve immediately.

SWEET POTATO PURÉE

1 lb. Moloka'i sweet potatoes	¼ cup heavy cream
¼ cup butter	Salt to taste
¼ cup milk	

Peel Moloka'i sweet potatoes, cut into quarters, and cook them quickly in boiling salted water ❧ When cooked, drain them and pass them quickly through a food mill ❧ Place in a pot and vigorously mix butter into purée ❧ Stir in boiling milk and cream a little at a time until the right consistency is reached ❧ Season to taste with salt ❧ Reheat, but do not allow to overheat ❧ Serve immediately.

(Recipes continue on page 97)

QUILCEDA CREEK
1995
WASHINGTON
CABERNET SAUVIGNON

ALBINI
FAMILY VINEYARDS

SONOMA COUNTY
19 Merlot 96

Moshin Vineyard
1996 PINOT NOIR
Russian River Valley

MIETZ
19
MERLOT

Franzen Photography

BRAISED ENDIVE

2   large Belgian endives   Salt and white pepper to taste
3   Tbsp. butter   Pinch of sugar
Chicken stock or water to cover

Remove any discolored outer leaves from the endives; cut off the root end and any green on top. Cut in half lengthwise. Put the butter in a large pan and gently sweat off the endive for a few minutes without coloring. Add the stock to barely cover and continue to cook on high heat, until the stock and butter have evaporated to a glaze and endive is cooked. Season to taste with salt, white pepper and sugar.

PICKLED GINGER PLUM SAUCE

1   cup kiawe honey   2   Tbsp. red wine vinegar   1   cup chicken broth
12   oz. red plums, pitted, cut   1   Tbsp. pickled ginger   Salt and white pepper to taste
     into 6 pieces

In a saucepan over medium-high heat, cook the honey and plums to a bright caramel color. Add red wine vinegar and pickled ginger and reduce for a few minutes, then add chicken broth. Bring to a boil for 5 minutes. Season to taste. Blend the sauce in a mixer, then strain the sauce after completed. Set aside and keep warm.

ROTISSERIE ISLAND CHICKEN

With "Huli-Huli" Style Sauce and Kahuku Cream Corn

SERVES 2

1 Island chicken, whole roaster	Pepper to taste	½ cup milk
½ cup Huli-Huli sauce (Pacific Poultry brand)	1 tsp. chopped garlic	"Huli-Huli" Style Sauce (see recipe below)
1 Tbsp. Hawaiian salt	1 Tbsp. butter	
	2 ears Kahuku corn, removed from the cob	

Brush chicken with Huli-Huli sauce ஃ Season with Hawaiian salt and pepper, hang in the oven, and roast at 375°F ஃ Brush with Huli-Huli sauce while baking ஃ Sauté garlic in butter, add corn, and sauté until translucent ஃ Cover with milk and simmer for 10 minutes ஃ Save half of the corn and blend the other half to a smooth consistency ஃ Mix with the whole corn and finish with butter ஃ Season to taste ஃ Remove the breasts and legs of the chicken from the bone ஃ Present on two individual plates, breast and leg on top of the cream corn surrounded with the "Huli-Huli" Style Sauce.

"HULI-HULI" STYLE SAUCE

1 tsp. minced shallots	1 Tbsp. salad oil	½ cup Huli-Huli sauce (Pacific Poultry brand)
1 tsp. chopped garlic	1 cup plum wine	
1 tsp. chopped ginger	½ cup demi-glace	1 finger chili pepper (local), minced
1 tsp. black pepper, cracked		1 tsp. sesame oil

In a saucepan sauté shallots, garlic, ginger and black pepper in salad oil ஃ Add plum wine and reduce to dry ஃ Stir in demi-glace, Huli-Huli sauce and chili pepper ஃ Finish with the sesame oil, then strain.

Crispy Ōpakapaka

DANIEL DELBREL | SHERATON MOANA SURFRIDER

BROILED OPAH

With Spinach, Thyme Lemongrass Sauce and Asian Tomato Salsa

SERVES 4

2 lbs. spinach, fresh leaves	24 oz. opah (6 oz. per serving)	Asian Tomato Salsa (see recipe
Salt and pepper to taste	Thyme Lemongrass Sauce (see	below)
	recipe below)	

Rinse spinach and blanch in boiling water; drain well ❧ Season with salt and pepper; set aside ❧ Season opah with salt and pepper and cook to desired doneness ❧ Place the warm spinach on a serving plate and top with the cooked opah ❧ Pour the Thyme Lemongrass Sauce over the opah and spoon Asian Tomato Salsa on top ❧ Serve immediately.

THYME LEMONGRASS SAUCE

6 oz. chicken stock	1 tsp. finely chopped lemongrass
2 oz. finely chopped shallots	2 tsp. butter
1 tsp. chopped fresh thyme	

In a saucepan combine chicken stock, shallots, thyme and lemongrass ❧ Bring to a boil and cook about 2 minutes or until mixture thickens.

ASIAN TOMATO SALSA

6 oz. diced tomato, seedless	½ oz. rice vinegar	⅛ tsp. Thai chili sauce or Tabasco
1 oz. finely chopped Maui onion	¼ tsp. grated ginger	Salt as needed
¼ tsp. chopped garlic	1 tsp. chopped Chinese parsley	

In a bowl combine all ingredients; mix well and keep refrigerated.

CASSEROLE OF PRAWNS

SERVES 2

1 Tbsp. olive oil	1 cup white wine	1 Tbsp. flour
½ Tbsp. chopped garlic	½ cup clam juice	Salt and pepper to taste
½ Tbsp. chopped shallots	½ cup heavy cream	10 prawns
1 tsp. paprika	3 Tbsp. butter	Panko Topping (see recipe below)

In a skillet heat olive oil and sauté garlic and shallots until translucent. Stir in paprika and white wine; reduce by half. Add clam juice and heavy cream; reduce by half. In a small skillet melt butter and stir in flour; blend until smooth. Add to sauce mixture and cook until thickened. Season with salt and pepper. Heat oil in a skillet and sauté prawns until done. Place in a serving dish, pour a little sauce over the prawns, and sprinkle with Panko Topping. Serve immediately.

PANKO TOPPING

1 cup panko	1 tsp. paprika
2 Tbsp. melted butter	1 tsp. chopped parsley
1 Tbsp. chopped garlic	

Preheat oven to 350°F. Combine panko, melted butter, garlic, paprika and parsley; blend well. Spread mixture on a baking sheet and bake until light brown.

ERIC FAIVRE | THE ORCHID AT MAUNA LANI

CRISPY 'ŌPAKAPAKA

With Oyster Mushroom Polenta, Hanaunau Beet Coulis and Wasabi Cream

SERVES 6

2¼ lb. Hawaiian 'ōpakapaka
    (Hawaiian pink snapper)
Salt and pepper to taste
2 Tbsp. olive oil
Oyster Mushroom Polenta (see
    recipe on next page)

Hanaunau Beet Coulis (see recipe
    below)
6 bunches micro watercress
Wasabi Cream (see recipe on next
    page)

Cut 'ōpakapaka into six 6-ounce filets ⁂ Season fish with salt and pepper ⁂ Sauté in olive oil ⁂ Do not overcook as the Hawaiian pink snapper is best when served medium ⁂ Place the Oyster Mushroom Polenta in the center of a large plate ⁂ Top with the pink snapper and a small bunch of micro watercress ⁂ Pour the Hanaunau Beet Coulis around the plate ⁂ Drizzle with Wasabi Cream.

HANAUNAU BEET COULIS

8 oz. fresh organic red beets
1 small Maui onion, chopped
1 tsp. chopped garlic

1 tsp. olive oil
½ cup cabernet sauvignon
2 cups chicken stock

1 Tbsp. white wine vinegar
Salt and pepper to taste

Peel the beets and cut into quarters ⁂ In a saucepan sauté Maui onion and garlic in olive oil ⁂ Deglaze the pan with red wine and reduce ⁂ Add beets and chicken stock and simmer until the beets are tender ⁂ Purée beets and add the vinegar ⁂ Season to taste with salt and pepper ⁂ The coulis needs to have a light consistency.

ERIC FAIVRE | THE ORCHID AT MAUNA LANI

OYSTER MUSHROOM POLENTA

1   Tbsp. chopped onion
1   tsp. butter
1½ cups chicken stock
4   oz. polenta

2   Tbsp. heavy cream
1   Tbsp. butter, softened
Salt and pepper to taste

4   oz. oyster mushrooms
1   Tbsp. olive oil
2   Tbsp. chopped chives

Sauté onion in butter. Add chicken stock and bring to a simmer. Stir in polenta and keep stirring until the polenta is soft. Add cream and butter and season to taste. Cut the oyster mushrooms in half lengthwise and toss with olive oil, salt and pepper. Slow roast at 250°F for 4 to 5 minutes or until soft. Drain and reserve the juices. Mix the mushrooms into the cooked polenta and stir in chives for color.

WASABI CREAM

3   Tbsp. sour cream
2   tsp. wasabi paste
1   tsp. lemon juice

1   tsp. chopped chives
Salt and pepper to taste

In a bowl combine sour cream, wasabi paste, lemon juice and chives; blend well. Season to taste with salt and pepper.

FRESH KONA LOBSTER

With Pineapple Curry Sauce

SERVES 2

2 Kona lobster or Maine lobster (1½ lbs. each)
2 large potatoes
½ Tbsp. butter
Pinch of salt and pepper

½ Tbsp. Thai yellow curry paste
1 Tbsp. vegetable oil
2 cups coconut milk
1 cup chicken or vegetable stock

4 oz. pineapple chunks (fresh or canned)
1 Tbsp. fish sauce or low-sodium soy sauce
Dash of sugar

Clean the lobsters by separating the body from the head; remove the brain and all the legs. Try to keep the heads in a whole piece to use for garnish. Cut the body in half from top to bottom; set aside. Prepare mashed potatoes by steaming or baking the potatoes until cooked, normally about 10 to 15 minutes depending on the temperature. Remove the skin and mash. Add butter, salt and pepper; set aside. In a pan sauté Thai yellow curry paste with the vegetable oil for a minute, then stir in coconut milk. Bring to a boil, then reduce heat and simmer for about 5 minutes. At this point you may add some chicken stock or water to thin the sauce down to the same consistency it was before you simmered it. Return heat to high and add lobster, pineapple, fish sauce and sugar. Continue cooking for about three minutes or until the lobster is cooked. Make sure you do not overcook the lobster. Use a large plate for presentation. Place a scoop of mashed potatoes in the middle of the plate, then put the head of the lobster standing up on top of the potatoes. Place the body and the claw on each side and drizzle with the sauce.

Kyle Rothenborg

GOUJONETTES ISLAND 'ŌPAKAPAKA

With Lemongrass Coconut Cream

SERVES 8

1   lb. fresh spinach leaves,
      rinsed and cut in 1" strips
2   Tbsp. butter
Lemongrass Coconut Cream
      (see recipe below)

3   lbs. Island snapper filet,
      cut in 4"x1" strip
      (3 pcs., 5 oz., per
      person)
Salt, pepper and lemon juice
      to taste

Flour for dusting
Garnish:
4   oz. seaweed (ogo), dusted with
      cornstarch and fried crisp
Pickled red ginger strips
Glazed Sweet Potato Slices (see

Sauté fresh spinach leaves in butter until wilted ❧ Add Lemongrass Coconut Cream; blend well ❧ Season fish filets with salt, pepper and lemon juice to taste ❧ Dust with flour ❧ Sear in a hot pan quickly ❧ Ladle creamed spinach in the middle of a plate and top with snapper ❧ Decorate with a crisp-fried seaweed fan, red ginger strips and 3 pieces of Glazed Sweet Potato Slices.

LEMONGRASS COCONUT CREAM

YIELD 1 QUART

1   cup white wine
3   cups coconut milk
1   cup chopped lemongrass

½   cup chopped shallots
¼   cup chopped ginger
1   cup heavy cream

1   cup thick béchamel sauce
Salt, pepper and lemon juice to
      taste

In a saucepan combine white wine, coconut milk, lemongrass, shallots and ginger; bring to a boil and reduce by half ❧ Strain through a fine sieve ❧ Stir in heavy cream and béchamel sauce ❧ Season to taste with salt, pepper and lemon juice.

GLAZED SWEET POTATO SLICES

24   slices (¼" thick) purple sweet potatoes
4   oz. melted butter
4   oz. maple syrup

Preheat oven to 350°F ❧ Blanch sweet potatoes, then drain and arrange in a single layer on a sheet pan ❧ Drizzle with melted butter and maple syrup ❧ Bake for 7 minutes.

GLENN CHU | INDIGO EURASIAN CUISINE

HAWAIIAN PLANTATIONS SHRIMP

With Liliko'i Kaffir Dressing

SERVES 4

1	tsp. black peppercorns	4	Tbsp. Heaven and Earth Dragon Fire Sauce	1½	tsp. salt
1	tsp. coriander seeds			½	cup olive oil
¼	cup liliko'i concentrate	1	Tbsp. minced fresh garlic	24	large Hawaiian plantations shrimp or white shrimp,
⅛	cup lime juice	2	kaffir leaves, finely minced		peeled and deveined
		½	bunch cilantro, chopped		

Prepare liliko'i kaffir dressing by first toasting peppercorns and coriander seeds. Cool, then grind to a powder. In a blender or food processor combine liliko'i concentrate, lime juice, 2 tablespoons of the Heaven and Earth Dragon Fire Sauce, peppercorn powder mixture, garlic, kaffir leaves, cilantro and salt. Turn on blender, then slowly add oil and mix until smooth. Preheat grill, brush shrimp with the remaining 2 tablespoons of the Dragon Fire Sauce and cook shrimp for 2 minutes on each side. Serve immediately with liliko'i kaffir dressing.

HERB-CRUSTED AMA EBI

With Warm Oyster Mushroom Potato Salad

SERVES 6

12 prawns (ama ebi), shelled and deveined (save shells)
Egg whites, lightly frothed
¼ cup chopped mixed herbs (basil, tarragon, parsley)

2 Tbsp. olive oil
¼ cup sherry vinegar
1 cup Shrimp Stock (see recipe below)
2 Tbsp. butter

Juice of one lemon
Salt and pepper to taste
Warm Oyster Mushroom Potato Salad (see recipe on next page)

Lightly coat prawns in egg wash and dredge in mixed herbs. In a sauté pan over medium heat, cook prawns in olive oil for 2 minutes. Remove prawns from pan and deglaze with sherry vinegar. Let reduce until dry, then add Shrimp Stock and bring to a boil. Reduce heat and swirl in butter. Season with lemon juice, salt and pepper. In the middle of a shallow bowl, place a generous spoonful of the warm potato salad. Ladle on shrimp sauce and top with two prawns.

SHRIMP STOCK

¼ cup diced onion
1 carrot, diced
½ stalk celery, diced
2 Tbsp. olive oil

Shells from prawns
¼ cup white wine
1 Tbsp. tomato paste
2½ cups water or fish stock

1 bay leaf
2 sprigs thyme
5 peppercorns, crushed

In a stockpot over medium heat sauté onions, carrot and celery in olive oil until lightly caramelized. Add prawn shells and stir until shells turn pink. Deglaze with white wine and reduce until dry. Stir in tomato paste, then add liquid and spices. Bring to a boil and reduce to a simmer for about 30 minutes. Strain liquid, making sure to press down on the solids in order to extract all the flavor. Return liquid to a saucepan and over medium-low heat let reduce until liquid yields 1½ cups.

DAVE REARDON | W HONOLULU—DIAMOND HEAD

WARM OYSTER MUSHROOM POTATO SALAD

4	medium fingerling potatoes, cooked, cut in half and sliced	6	Tbsp. olive oil	4	cups oyster mushrooms or assorted mushrooms, sliced
1	Moloka'i sweet potato, cooked and diced	½	cup roasted red and yellow bell pepper, seeded, julienne	¼	cup chopped shallots
			Salt and pepper to taste	2	Tbsp. chopped garlic

In a sauté pan over medium heat, sauté fingerling and sweet potatoes in 2 tablespoons of the olive oil until golden brown ≈ Add roasted bell peppers ≈ Season to taste with salt and pepper ≈ Keep warm ≈ In a sauté pan over medium-high heat, cook mushrooms in the remaining 4 tablespoons olive oil in small batches until golden brown ≈ Toss in shallots and garlic at the end of each batch and season with salt and pepper ≈ Mix potatoes and mushrooms together gently and keep warm.

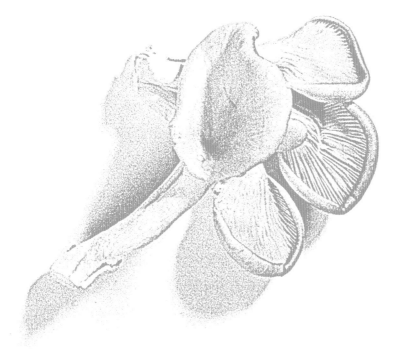

HOT BEAN SALMON ALLA SICILIANA

With Risotto

SERVES 4

1¼ lb. salmon filet	Risotto (see recipe on next page)	Crispy deep-fried noodles for
Hot Bean Marinade (see recipe below)	Sauce (see recipe on next page)	garnish, if desired

Cut salmon at an angle into four filets ❧ Brush a little Hot Bean Marinade on both sides of filets and marinate overnight (Do not soak salmon in marinade——a little goes a long way.) ❧ Spray salmon with nonstick spray and broil to mark ❧ Finish in the oven until done (Salmon can be panfried as well.) ❧ Place a small amount of Risotto in the middle of a plate and top with salmon ❧ Mix Sauce well to incorporate before using ❧ Pour Sauce over salmon, letting Sauce drizzle down the sides ❧ Garnish with crispy deep-fried noodles and serve with a green salad of your choice.

HOT BEAN MARINADE

MAKES 3 CUPS

8	oz. hot bean sauce	2	oz. honey	2	tsp. black pepper
2	oz. garlic, chopped	4	oz. sherry	8	oz. olive oil
2	oz. shallots, chopped				

Combine all ingredients and mix well.

RISOTTO

2	Tbsp. extra virgin olive oil	1	Tbsp. chopped garlic	5	cups chicken broth
4	Tbsp. butter	1	cup white wine	½	cup grated Parmesan cheese
1	small round onion, diced	1½	cups arborio rice		Salt and pepper to taste

In a saucepan with a heavy bottom heat olive oil and 2 tablespoons of the butter and sauté onion and garlic until onions are translucent ✦ Add wine and reduce by half ✦ Add rice and stir for approximately 2 minutes ✦ Add chicken broth slowly, stirring until all the broth is absorbed before adding more ✦ Reduce heat to low, cook for 20 minutes, stirring occasionally ✦ Taste for firm but tender consistency ✦ Stir in Parmesan cheese and remaining 2 tablespoons of the butter; cook for 3 minutes ✦ Season to taste with salt and pepper ✦ Serve immediately.

SAUCE

MAKES ABOUT 3 CUPS

5	oz. fish sauce	2	oz. chopped garlic	1	tsp. salt or to taste
5	oz. balsamic vinegar	2	oz. chili garlic sauce	1	anise seed, crushed and chopped
5	oz. rice vinegar	¾	cup sugar	½	tsp. Chinese five spice
1	cup olive oil				

Combine all ingredients in a food processor or mix at low speed with an immersion blender.

ALAN TSUCHIYAMA | SHERATON WAIKĪKĪ

MACADAMIA NUT-CRUSTED MAHIMAHI

With Chili Coconut Butter Sauce, Sesame Potato Cakes and Sautéed Spinach

SERVES 4

1 cup panko (Japanese bread crumbs)
⅓ cup chopped macadamia nuts
2 tsp. grated ginger
4 mahimahi filets (6 oz. each)
Salt and pepper to taste

Oil or butter for sautéing
Sesame Potato Cakes (see recipe below)
Sautéed Spinach (see recipe on next page)
Chili Coconut Butter Sauce (see recipe on next page)

In a food processor combine panko, macadamia nuts and ginger and chop until fine ✎ Season mahimahi with salt and pepper, then cover filets with macadamia nut crust ✎ Sauté fish in oil or butter until golden brown and fish flakes easily when tested with a fork ✎ Place a Sesame Potato Cake in the center of a plate and top with Sautéed Spinach ✎ Place mahimahi on the spinach and drizzle with Chili Coconut Butter Sauce.

SESAME POTATO CAKES

3 medium baking potatoes
¼ cup julienne carrot
¼ cup julienne zucchini

¼ cup julienne Maui onion
2 Tbsp. sour cream
1½ tsp. black sesame seeds

1½ tsp. toasted white sesame seeds
Salt and pepper to taste
Oil for sautéing

Bake potatoes at 425°F for 35 to 40 minutes or until pierced easily with skewer ✎ Cool potatoes, then peel and grate ✎ In a skillet sauté carrot, zucchini and Maui onion until tender ✎ Combine potatoes, carrot, zucchini, Maui onion, sour cream, and black and white sesame seeds; blend well ✎ Season to taste with salt and pepper ✎ Form into four patties ✎ Sauté in oil until golden brown on both sides.

ALAN TSUCHIYAMA | SHERATON WAIKIKI

SAUTÉED SPINACH

1   Tbsp. chopped shallots   8   oz. fresh spinach leaves, rinsed
1   Tbsp. butter   Salt and pepper to taste

Sweat shallots in butter until transparent ⁂ Sauté spinach until wilted ⁂ Season with salt and pepper.

CHILI COCONUT BUTTER SAUCE

½ cup white wine   ½ cup unsweetened coconut milk   ½ tsp. sweet Thai chili sauce
½ cup heavy whipping cream   1 tsp. finely chopped shallots   1 tsp. chopped basil
½ cup chicken broth   ½ tsp. minced ginger   2 Tbsp. soft butter (not melted)

In a small saucepan combine white wine, heavy cream, chicken broth, coconut milk, shallots and ginger ⁂ Simmer and reduce to about ⅓ cup ⁂ Add chili sauce and basil ⁂ Slowly whisk in butter, until all the butter is melted and incorporated into the sauce.

JAMES MCDONALD | I'O

MACADAMIA COCONUT-CRUSTED FISH

With Thai Peanut Sauce, Sweet Sour Glaze and Tropical Fruit Salsa

SERVES 4

1 cup finely chopped
    macadamia nuts
½ cup unsweetened coconut
    thread
¼ cup panko (Japanese
    bread crumbs)
½ cup flour
2 eggs, beaten
4 mahimahi or salmon filets
    (5 oz. each)
Salt and pepper to taste
4 Tbsp. peanut oil

In a shallow pan combine macadamia nuts, coconut and panko; mix well ❧ Place flour in another shallow pan and eggs in a third shallow pan ❧ ONLY bread one side of fish ❧ Dip fish filets in flour, then eggs, and then nut mixture ❧ Season fish with salt and pepper ❧ In a sauté pan heat peanut oil and sauté fish, nut side down, and cook until golden brown ❧ Turn fish over, remove from heat, and cover with lid until ready to serve.

Tony Novak-Clifford

JAMES McDONALD | I'O

Presentation: Place a small, flat mound of rice on center of each plate. Ladle Thai Peanut Sauce around rice. Place fish on top of rice; ladle just enough Sweet Sour Glaze to coat the fish. Top fish with Tropical Fruit Salsa and serve.

THAI PEANUT SAUCE

1	oz. lemongrass, chopped semi-fine	2	oz. lime juice	1	cup coconut milk	
1	oz. ginger, roughly chopped	4	oz. sake	2	cups peanut butter	
1	oz. garlic, roughly chopped	1	oz. shrimp sauce	1	tsp. sambal chili paste	
		1	cup chicken stock	Salt to taste		

In a sauce pot over medium heat, dry sauté the lemongrass, ginger and garlic for one minute. Next add lime juice, sake and shrimp sauce. Reduce by half. Add chicken stock and reduce by half. Add coconut milk and peanut butter and let simmer 15 minutes. Strain; add sambal and salt to taste.

SWEET SOUR GLAZE

1	cup sugar	2	tsp. ground cinnamon	¼	cup white wine vinegar	
1	oz. low-sodium soy sauce	¼	cup red wine vinegar	2	cinnamon sticks	
2	cups rice wine vinegar	2	tsp. red chili flakes			

In a sauce pot over medium heat combine all ingredients. Bring to a boil, then reduce heat to low and simmer for 20 minutes, stirring occasionally.

TROPICAL FRUIT SALSA

½	cup diced pineapple	½	cup diced mango	2	Tbsp. roughly chopped cilantro	
½	cup diced papaya	¼	cup diced onion			

Combine all ingredients together; mix well. Set aside and chill.

MAI TAI MAHIMAHI

With Kula Greens and Kona Coffee Glaze

SERVES 20

8   lbs. mahimahi
Baby greens
Crispy croutons
Cure Mixture (see recipe below)
Mai Tai Marinade (see recipe below)
Kona Coffee Glaze (see recipe below)

Coat 2 sides of mahimahi (about 8 lbs.) with Cure Mixture for 18 to 24 hours. Rinse filets and air-dry for 4 hours. Marinate cured fish in Mai Tai Marinade for 12 hours. Remove from marinade and air-dry for 4 hours. Trim out bloodline and slice on the bias into paper-thin slices. Lightly pound if needed. Place on parchment paper and reserve until ready to serve.

Presentation: Layer baby greens and crispy croutons on a plate. Top with mahimahi slices and drizzle with Kona Coffee Glaze. Garnish with edible flowers.

Chef's Suggestion: Other firm white fish can be substituted for mahimahi.

CURE MIXTURE

1½ cups salt
2   cups sugar
2   Tbsp. cracked black pepper

Combine all ingredients and blend well.

MAI TAI MARINADE

1   cup Malibu rum
1   cup dark rum
2½ cups orange juice
1½ cups pineapple juice
½   cup grenadine

Combine all ingredients and blend well.

KONA COFFEE GLAZE

½   cup 100% Kona coffee
1   Tbsp. macadamia nuts, toasted and chopped
1   cup dark brown sugar
¼   cup Pommery whole-grain mustard
2   Tbsp. chopped fresh dill

Combine all ingredients and blend well.

DAVID PAUL JOHNSON | DAVID PAUL'S LAHAINA GRILL

MAUI ONION-CRUSTED SEARED 'AHI

With Vanilla Bean Rice, Caramelized Onions and Apple Cider Soy Butter Vinaigrette

SERVES 4

1 cup jasmine rice
1 vanilla bean, split in half lengthwise
1 Tbsp. finely chopped shallots
1 Tbsp. butter
4 oz. dry white wine
2½ cups fish or clam broth
2 cups apple cider vinegar
2 cups filtered apple cider

2 oz. unsalted butter, chilled and cubed
½ lb. soy margarine, chilled and cubed
1 lb. Maui onions, thinly sliced, tossed in 1 tsp. oil, salt and black pepper
3 Tbsp. olive oil
Salt and pepper

1 lb. premium 'ahi filet, cut into 2" x 2" strips
¾ lb. Maui onions, peeled, sliced thin, dehydrated and crushed into powder (allow dehydrated onions to dry for 24 hours)
1 oz. chives, chopped fine
1 Tbsp. black sesame seeds

In a saucepan lightly glaze the rice over medium heat with vanilla bean, shallots and butter. Deglaze with the white wine, then add broth. Bring to a slow boil, then reduce heat to a simmer. Cover and let simmer until all liquid is absorbed, approximately 20 minutes. Remove from heat and fluff. In a saucepan combine vinegar and apple cider, then reduce over medium heat until ½ cup is left.

Right before service, add chilled unsalted butter and margarine cubes in small quantities while mixing sauce over medium heat. Place in a blender and pulse for just a second or two. In a heavy-bottomed saucepan over medium-high heat cook the tossed sliced onions in 2 Tbsp. of the olive oil, stirring constantly, until onions are evenly caramelized. Season with salt and pepper. Set aside. In a large skillet heat the remaining 1 Tbsp. olive oil. Roll 'ahi filets in onion powder and salt and pepper. Sear fish on four sides until just browned but rare in the center. At service, slice fish against the grain into ½"-thick slices. Place each serving of fish on top of an arranged mound of rice in the center of a large plate. Top with a tablespoon of caramelized onions. Drizzle ¼ of the sauce around and on top of the fish. Garnish with chives and black sesame seeds.

ONAGA BAKED IN A THYME AND ROSEMARY ROCK SALT CRUST

With Fresh Herb and Ogo Sauce

SERVES 2

2 lb. whole onaga (red snapper)	Salt and pepper to taste	Fresh Herb and Ogo Sauce (see
1 lb. spinach leaves	2 ti leaves, large	recipe on next page)
3 cloves garlic, finely chopped	Rosemary Rock Salt Crust (see	
3 Tbsp. olive oil	recipe below)	

Ask your butcher to remove the filets from the onaga, keeping the skin on ⁊ Sauté spinach and garlic in olive oil ⁊ Season to taste with salt and pepper and cool in the refrigerator for a few minutes ⁊ Place ti leaves on the Rosemary Rock Salt Crust to protect the fish from the salt (the top of the fish will be protected by the skin) ⁊ Arrange the spinach on the ti leaves with the two filets skin up, lying side by side, on the top of the spinach ⁊ Wrap the onaga in the salt crust dough and shape the dough like a fish ⁊ Bake in oven for 25 minutes at 375°F ⁊ To serve, cut the crust lengthwise, removing only the top of the crust (Extra caution should be taken so that no salt crystals fall onto the fish.) ⁊ Remove the skin from the fish ⁊ On individual plates, place the spinach on top of the fish and arrange the herb sauce around the fish.

ROSEMARY ROCK SALT CRUST

2 lbs. all-purpose flour	1 Tbsp. dried rosemary	3 egg whites, lightly beaten
1 lb. rock salt	1 Tbsp. dried thyme	1 cup water

In a mixing bowl sift flour ⁊ Add rock salt, rosemary, thyme and egg whites and ½ cup of the water ⁊ Mix until a stiff dough is formed, adding the remaining water as needed ⁊ Roll out the dough thin enough to wrap the fish.

GEORGE MAVROTHALASSITIS | CHEF MAVRO

FRESH HERB AND OGO SAUCE

2   shallots, finely chopped
6   Tbsp. olive oil
3   garlic cloves, finely chopped
½   cup white wine
1   tomato, peeled, seeded and diced

1   sprig tarragon, finely chopped
1   sprig chervil, finely chopped
2   Tbsp. green onion, finely
      chopped

½   cup ogo, finely chopped
      (Hawaiian seaweed)
Salt and pepper to taste

In a saucepan sauté shallots in olive oil for a few minutes. Do not brown the shallots. Add garlic and white wine and reduce to half. Add all the remaining ingredients. Finish with olive oil. Season to taste with salt and pepper.

Dana Edmunds

ROASTED KEĀHOLE LOBSTER AND WAIMEA BOUQUET OF GREENS

With Moloka'i Sweet Potato Purée

SERVES 2

1½ lb. Keāhole lobster, whole, live	1½ Tbsp. extra virgin olive oil	2 sprigs mâche
1 qt. nage (vegetable and white wine stock)	Salt and pepper to taste	2 sprigs tango lettuce (or arugula and green leaf lettuce)
½ Tbsp. lemon juice	Moloka'i Sweet Potato Purée (see recipe below)	
	Mango Sauce (see recipe below)	

Poach lobster in the nage for 8 minutes ✒ Leave the shell on the tail ✒ Cut the tail into halves lengthwise ✒ Remove the shell from the claws and knuckles ✒ Combine lemon juice, olive oil, salt and pepper ✒ Brush lobster with part of the dressing ✒ Charbroil a few minutes just before serving ✒ Arrange Moloka'i Sweet Potato Purée in the center of the plate ✒ Surround with the Mango Sauce ✒ Arrange the lobster tail, claw and knuckles on the top; finish with the bouquet of lettuces tossed with the remaining dressing.

MOLOKA'I SWEET POTATO PURÉE

1 large Moloka'i sweet potato	½ cup milk
1 Hawaiian vanilla bean	2 Tbsp. butter

Bake whole sweet potato in oven at 450°F for 40 minutes ✒ Pass through a food mill ✒ Cut the Hawaiian vanilla bean in half lengthwise and remove seeds ✒ In a saucepan heat milk and add vanilla seeds ✒ In a mixing bowl combine sweet potato with milk mixture and finish with butter.

MANGO SAUCE

1 medium mango, ripe	1 tsp. sherry vinegar	Salt, pepper and sugar (if mangoes
½ cup water	1 Tbsp. salad oil	are not ripe enough) to taste

Combine all ingredients and blend well.

DOUG LUM | MARIPOSA

SAUTÉED ʻŌPAKAPAKA

With a Lively Three Pepper Vinaigrette

SERVES 4

2   lbs. ʻōpakapaka filet, pin bones removed
¼   lb. unsalted butter
1   cup white wine
1   cup rice wine vinegar
1   tsp. minced shallot

Pinch of salt
Pinch of black pepper, white pepper and cayenne pepper
½   tsp. paprika
¼   cup whipping cream

12   oz. Yukon gold potatoes
2   Tbsp. lemon juice
Flour for dusting
Olive oil for sautéing
12   oz. seasonal vegetables, cooked

Cut ʻōpakapaka into four equal portions and set aside ❧ Cut butter into pieces about a quarter inch thick and let sit out at room temperature ❧ In a sauce pot combine wine, vinegar, shallot, salt, the three peppers and paprika ❧ Place the pot over high heat and reduce mixture until syrupy ❧ Add whipping cream and reduce by 60 percent ❧ Reduce the heat to low and slowly whisk in butter ❧ At this point the sauce should be kept in a warm place and not allowed to cool or get too hot ❧ Slice potatoes lengthwise into wedges and baste with lemon juice, then roast until golden brown ❧ While the potatoes are cooking, heat a sauté pan over high heat ❧ Dust ʻōpakapaka with flour and sauté in olive oil until golden brown ❧ Place the roasted potato spears in the middle of the plate ❧ Place a portion of cooked seasonal vegetables on top of the potatoes and top with a fish filet ❧ Coat fish with the sauce and drizzle some more sauce around the plate for color.

GREG GASPAR | THE WESTIN MAUI PRINCE HOTEL MAKENA

SEARED 'AHI TOWER

With Foie Gras and Creamy Polenta

SERVES 2

¼ tsp. black peppercorns	½ tsp. ground star anise	4 cups veal stock
¼ tsp. red whole peppercorns	8 oz. chicken stock	2 cups port wine
¼ tsp. green whole peppercorns	2 Tbsp. chopped shallots	4 tsp. olive oil
¼ tsp. Szechwan peppercorns	½ cup cornmeal (polenta)	4 oz. raw spinach
5 oz. 'ahi, sashimi grade, blocked	½ cup sliced shiitake mushrooms	Salt and pepper to taste
3 oz. foie gras	8 oz. heavy cream	2 tsp. beurre blanc
1 tsp. salt	3 Tbsp. unsalted butter	4 tube chives

In a sauté pan toast peppercorns lightly on medium heat. Set aside to cool. When cool, place peppercorns in a spice grinder and grind to a fine consistency. Lightly season 'ahi block with pepper mixture. Season foie gras with salt and star anise. Set 'ahi and foie gras aside. In a saucepan bring chicken stock to a simmer, then add 1 tablespoon of the chopped shallots, corn meal (polenta) and shiitake mushrooms. Cook for three minutes. Finish with heavy cream and slowly stir in butter; set aside. In a small saucepan combine veal stock, the remaining 1 tablespoon chopped shallots and port wine; reduce by half and strain. Season to taste with salt and pepper. In a medium sauté pan on high heat, add 2 teaspoons of the olive oil and sear 'ahi for 2 to 3 seconds quickly on all four sides; set aside. In a small sauté pan, sear foie gras on both sides until medium rare; set aside. In a medium sauté pan heat 2 teaspoons olive oil and sauté spinach for a few minutes. Season to taste with salt and pepper; set aside. Place creamy polenta in middle of plate and top with sautéed spinach. Cut seared 'ahi block diagonally and place on plate. Place foie gras on spinach, sauce with port wine reduction, and drizzle beurre blanc sauce on plate. Garnish with chives.

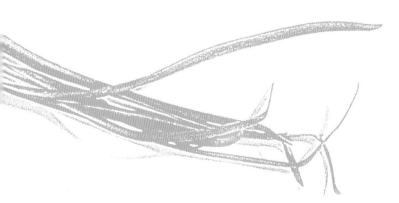

SEARED DIVER SCALLOPS

With Black Truffle Vinaigrette

SERVES 4

1   Tbsp. olive oil
1   Tbsp. minced garlic
2   Tbsp. minced fresh herbs
      (cilantro, basil, chervil)
Salt and pepper to taste
12 diver scallops
Cranberry Leek Compote (see
      recipe on next page)
Duck Confit Relish (see recipe
      on next page)
Black Truffle Vinaigrette (see
      recipe on next page)

Combine olive oil, garlic, fresh herbs, salt and pepper. Marinate scallops for several hours. Sear to medium-rare before serving. On your serving plate, set the scallops on top of the Cranberry Leek Compote and garnish the middle of the plate with the Duck Confit Relish. Finish with a drizzle of Black Truffle Vinaigrette.

Jon DeMello

ERIC FAIVRE | THE ORCHID AT MAUNA LANI

CRANBERRY LEEK COMPOTE

½ cup julienne leeks
2 Tbsp. olive oil
½ cup fresh cranberries
1 tsp. minced orange zest

1 tsp. minced lemon zest
1 cinnamon stick
¼ tsp. ground nutmeg

1 cup orange juice
2 oz. brown sugar
Salt and pepper to taste

Sauté leeks in olive oil until translucent. Add the remaining ingredients and cook down until thick. Adjust seasoning as needed.

DUCK CONFIT RELISH

1 cup duck confit
4 oz. thinly sliced purple
    cabbage
2 oz. julienne red onion

1 oz. pea sprouts
Black Truffle Vinaigrette to
    taste (see recipe below)

Salt and freshly ground pepper
    to taste

Combine duck confit, cabbage, onion and pea sprouts; blend well. Toss lightly with Black Truffle Vinaigrette and season to taste with salt and pepper.

BLACK TRUFFLE VINAIGRETTE

2 Tbsp. white wine vinegar
1 Tbsp. minced shallots
¼ Tbsp. minced garlic

2 Tbsp. extra virgin olive oil
2 Tbsp. black truffle oil
1 Tbsp. black truffle pieces

1 tsp. honey
Salt and freshly ground pepper to
    taste

In a blender combine vinegar, shallots and garlic. Slowly drizzle in oils to emulsify. Add truffle pieces and honey. Season to taste with salt and pepper.

BRYAN ASHLOCK | SHERATON MAUI KĀ'ANAPALI BEACH RESORT

SEARED ONAGA FLORENTINE

SERVES 2

2 oz. smoked bacon, diced	1 Tbsp. lemon juice	1 Tbsp. olive oil
¼ Maui onion, diced	1 tsp. salt	1 oz. white wine
8 oz. fresh spinach	1 tsp. pepper	1 oz. butter
2 oz. Beurre Blanc (see recipe below)	2 onaga or other snapper filets (6 oz. each)	½ Tbsp. chili tobiko or wasabi tobiko
½ Tbsp. Worcestershire sauce	½ cup flour	Parsley potatoes, if desired

Sauté diced bacon and cook to ¾ doneness. Add Maui onion and cook until transparent, approximately 30 to 45 seconds. Add fresh spinach and toss until wilted. Stir in Beurre Blanc and remove from heat; set aside. In a small bowl combine Worcestershire sauce, ½ tablespoon of the lemon juice, salt and pepper. Roll onaga filets in Worcestershire sauce mixture, then dust with flour. In a medium sauté pan heat the olive oil and sear the fish, until lightly brown on one side. Turn and cook a few more minutes. Deglaze the pan with the white wine. Add the remaining ½ tablespoon lemon juice and butter. Finish off in an oven preheated to 375°F for 6 to 8 minutes. Place spinach mixture on fish and sprinkle with chili tobiko for garnish. Serve with potatoes.

BEURRE BLANC

½ cup white wine	1 tsp. fish bouillon	1 cup heavy whipping cream
1 tablespoon Worcestershire sauce	½ tsp. lobster base	½ cup butter, chipped

In a small saucepan combine white wine, Worcestershire sauce, fish bouillon and lobster base; reduce. Reduce the whipping cream in a separate saucepan and combine to the first reduction. With wire whip gradually add butter chips; blend well.

STEAMED MOI, HAWAIIAN STYLE

SERVES 4

2   lbs. whole moi, scaled,
    cleaned and seasoned
½   cup peanut oil
3   cups shiitake, crimini,
    portabellini and chanterelle
    mushrooms, julienne

1   clove garlic, minced
½   cup ginger, fine julienne
1   cup cooked somen noodles
½   cup fine julienne carrots
½   cup fine julienne leeks
½   cup fine julienne bell peppers

⅓   cup fine julienne green onions
⅓   cup cilantro sprigs for garnish
¼   cup ponzu sauce
¼   cup soy sauce
2   Tbsp. sesame oil

In a nonstick pan heat 1 tablespoon of the peanut oil and sauté the mushrooms with garlic; set aside. Fillet the moi off the bone, leaving the head portion intact. Rub the exposed meat with garlic and stuff with ginger. Steam the moi, covered, for 7 to 12 minutes. When the moi is cooked, remove it from the steamer and place it on a serving plate on top of the somen noodles that have been mixed with the julienne vegetables. Sprinkle with green onions and cilantro. Place the mushrooms around the noodles. Combine ponzu sauce and soy sauce. Heat the remaining peanut oil and sesame oil. Finish by pouring the hot oils on the moi, then add 4 to 5 tablespoons of the ponzu mixture over all. Serve.

DAVID BOUCHER | HYATT REGENCY KAUA'I

TARO-CRUSTED HAWAIIAN 'ŌPAKAPAKA

SERVES 4

6	oz. Chinese taro (or potato)	1	Tbsp. cornstarch
12	oz. fresh 'ōpakapaka or other	2	eggs, lightly beaten
	snapper fillet		Oil for shallow frying
1	oz. flour		Liliko'i Red Curry Sauce
	Salt and pepper to taste		(see recipe below)
1	tsp. minced garlic		

Peel taro and julienne with knife or grater ❧ Soak overnight in water to help remove starch ❧ Cut fish into four 3-ounce pieces ❧ Combine flour, salt and pepper and spread on a plate ❧ Mix garlic and cornstarch with the well-drained taro ❧ Coat fish with flour, dip into egg and then taro ❧ In a sauté pan heat the oil and cook fish until cooked through ❧ Ladle Liliko'i Red Curry Sauce over fish to serve.

LILIKO'I RED CURRY SAUCE

1	qt. chicken stock	1	Tbsp. minced garlic	1	Tbsp. coarsely chopped parsley
¼	cup liliko'i purée	¼	cup brown sugar	3	Tbsp. cornstarch
2	Tbsp. red Thai curry paste	1	Tbsp. minced lemongrass	¼	cup heavy cream
2	Tbsp. coconut milk				

In a saucepan combine all ingredients, except cornstarch and heavy cream, and whisk vigorously ❧ Bring to a boil; reduce heat and simmer ❧ Combine cornstarch and heavy cream to make a slurry, then slowly add to the simmering sauce ❧ Cook until thickened.

TOGARASHI-GLAZED SALMON

SERVES 2

2   salmon filets (6 oz. each)
3   oz. Fish Marinade (see recipe below)
Salt and pepper to taste

2   oz. Sugar Crust (see recipe below)
1   oz. macadamia nut oil
2   oz. Grand Marnier

2   oz. soy sauce
Juice of 2 oranges
2   oz. unsalted butter

Cover salmon filets with marinade; reserve refrigerated for an hour ᴥ Heat a sauté pan over medium-high heat ᴥ Remove salmon from the marinade, season with salt and pepper, and dredge in Sugar Crust, skin side up ᴥ Add macadamia nut oil to the sauté pan ᴥ When it begins to smoke, carefully place the salmon, sugar side down, in the oil ᴥ Turn the heat down to medium; allow to cook for 30 seconds, carefully flipping salmon over, then deglazing the pan with the Grand Marnier, soy sauce and orange juice ᴥ Place into an oven preheated to 450°F for about 3 minutes ᴥ If you like your fish done medium, look for an internal temperature of about 120°F ᴥ Remove the salmon from the pan; with the heat turned off, add the butter to the pan drippings to make the sauce ᴥ Enjoy!

FISH MARINADE

1   oz. rice vinegar
1   oz. fresh lemon juice

1   tsp. minced garlic
1   tsp. finely grated ginger

Cilantro, coarsely chopped, no stem
1   oz. macadamia nut oil

Combine all ingredients, except the macadamia nut oil, and blend well ᴥ Slowly drizzle in the oil to emulsify.

SUGAR CRUST

2   oz. granulated sugar
2   oz. brown sugar
1   Tbsp. togarashi (Japanese chili seasoning)

Combine all ingredients together, blend well, and reserve.

VOLCANIC 'AHI

With Tropical Relish

SERVES 2

4   oz. block fresh Pacific big eye
    tuna or yellowtail
½   oz. Cajun spice
2   Tbsp. diced Maui onion or
    sweet onion
1   Tbsp. diced bell peppers
    (green, red and yellow bell
    peppers)
2   oz. diced celery

1   Yukon gold potato, peeled and
    diced
2   cloves garlic, finely minced
1   Tbsp. finely minced shallot
½   oz. olive oil
¼   tsp. fish bouillon powder
Salt and white pepper to taste
Juice of 1 lemon
1   tsp. Worcestershire sauce
3   oz. mayonnaise

4   fresh kumquats, skin only (no
    white), cut into fine julienne
1   sprig lemon thyme, finely
    minced
1   box phyllo sheets
Clarified butter
Tropical Relish (see recipe below)
6   sprigs fresh mint
⅛   tsp. dill
Pinch of chili pepper flakes

Dust fish with Cajun spice on all four sides. Sear in a hot skillet with a little olive oil until outside surface is caramelized, but fish is still raw on the inside. Dice into ¼-inch cubes and set aside. In a skillet sauté Maui onion, bell peppers, celery, potato, garlic and shallot in olive oil. Remove from heat when ingredients become transparent or half-cooked. Fold into seared cubed fish and season with fish bouillon powder, salt and white pepper. Add lemon juice and Worcestershire sauce; blend well. Stir in mayonnaise. Stir in kumquat and lemon thyme. Adjust seasoning. Lay out phyllo dough sheets, one at a time, brushing each sheet with clarified butter between layers. Layer three sheets, then add approximately 1½ ounces of seafood mixture and fold into a triangular shape. Bake at 375°F for approximately 12 to 15 minutes or until golden brown. Serve with Tropical Relish and garnish plate with sprigs of fresh mint, dill and chili pepper flakes.

TROPICAL RELISH

1   Maui pineapple
1   fresh Hayden mango
6   fresh lychee or rambutan

1   fresh papaya
2   mountain apples

1   Hawaiian chili pepper or
    habanero pepper, optional

Peel and dice all the fruit, then fold in finely minced chili pepper. Arrange on plate with Volcanic 'Ahi. All fruits may be substituted with local fruits in season.

DAVE REARDON | W HONOLULU–DIAMOND HEAD

WASABI POTATO CRUSTED 'ŌPAKAPAKA

With Thai Spiced Black Rice And Tomato Lobster Broth

SERVES 4

WASABI POTATO CRUSTED 'ŌPAKAPAKA

4   'ōpakapaka (snapper) filets,
    (7 oz. each)
Salt and pepper to taste
2   Tbsp. olive oil

2   potatoes, peeled
1   Tbsp. wasabi powder
Thai Spiced Black Rice (see recipe
    below)

Tomato Lobster Broth (see recipe
    on next page)

Season filets with salt and pepper ⬧ In a sauté pan heat olive oil ⬧ Shred the potatoes and place in a bowl ⬧ Add wasabi powder and mix well ⬧ Place the shredded potato on the top side of fish filets only ⬧ Sauté fish until potatoes are golden; turn over and finish cooking ⬧ To serve, place a portion of Thai Spiced Black Rice on a plate and top with fish filet ⬧ Lace with Tomato Lobster Broth.

THAI SPICED BLACK RICE

1   tsp. squid ink
2   cups water
1   cup Uncle Ben's converted rice
1   Tbsp. chopped cilantro

1   onion, diced
1   jalapeño pepper
1   bunch green onions, diced

1   tsp. minced ginger
1   tsp. minced garlic
Salt and pepper to taste

In a stock pot combine squid ink and water and bring to a boil ⬧ Stir in all the remaining ingredients ⬧ Cover and place in an oven preheated to 350°F for 20 minutes, stirring occasionally ⬧ Season to taste with salt and pepper ⬧ Set aside and keep warm until ready to serve.

TOMATO LOBSTER BROTH

2	Tbsp. olive oil	1	tsp. minced garlic	2	oz. tarragon
1	lb. lobster shells	1	Tbsp. tomato paste	½	cup white wine
1	onion, chopped	½	cup sun-dried tomatoes	1	quart water
1	bulb fennel, sliced	10	Roma tomatoes, chopped	2	Tbsp. lemon juice
2	leeks, sliced	2	oz. basil, chopped	Salt and pepper to taste	

In a stockpot heat olive oil and cook lobster shells until they become bright red. Add onion, fennel, leeks and garlic and sauté for five minutes. Add tomato paste and sauté. Add sun-dried tomatoes, Roma tomatoes and herbs and sauté for 10 minutes. Deglaze with white wine. Add water and lemon juice. Simmer for 45 minutes. Season to taste with salt and pepper, then pass through a fine sieve. Hold for service.

WOK-CHARRED 'AHI

SERVES 2

½ cup soybean oil	2 tsp. crushed garlic	Juice of ½ lemon
1 Tbsp. freshly grated ginger	1 tsp. dried marjoram	2 8-oz. 'ahi logs (cut 4" long by
2 Tbsp. chopped shallots	Pinch of cayenne pepper	1¼"), scored on top for
¼ tsp. crushed chilies	1 tsp. salt	cutting
¼ tsp. dried thyme		

In a bowl combine all ingredients, except 'ahi; mix well. Heat wok until metal begins turning white. Dredge 'ahi logs in coating mixture, then sear in wok 20 seconds on each side. Slice and serve.

Chef's Suggestion: The dipping sauce we use is 4 parts shoyu (soy sauce), 1 part mirin, 1 part lime juice and wasabi to taste. Wasabi must be made into a thick paste with water first. Use ¼ cup wasabi to 2 cups shoyu as a sashimi dip. Fresh tropical fruit makes an excellent accompaniment.

Chocolate Crunch Bars

SCOTT LUTEY | SHERATON KAUA'I RESORT

BANANA LUMPIA

SERVES 6

3 bananas, peeled
6 lumpia wrappers
¼ cup finely diced macadamia nuts
½ cup egg wash
2 cups oil for frying
6 scoops lychee ice cream (2 oz. each)
Anise Syrup (see recipe below)

Slice bananas in half crosswise ❧ Lay lumpia wrappers on work surface and sprinkle wrappers with macadamia nuts ❧ Place banana at one corner of wrapper and roll, pulling up sides like a burrito ❧ Seal edges with egg wash ❧ Preheat oil to 350°F and fry lumpia until golden brown ❧ Remove lumpia from oil and place on a paper towel to absorb excess oil ❧ Place a scoop of lychee ice cream in center of a plate ❧ Cut lumpia at an angle and arrange 3 pieces around ice cream ❧ Drizzle with Anise Syrup.

ANISE SYRUP

1 cup granulated sugar
½ cup water
2 whole star anise

In a small saucepan combine sugar, water and star anise and bring to a boil ❧ Reduce heat and simmer until sauce reaches a syrup consistency ❧ Strain and keep warm.

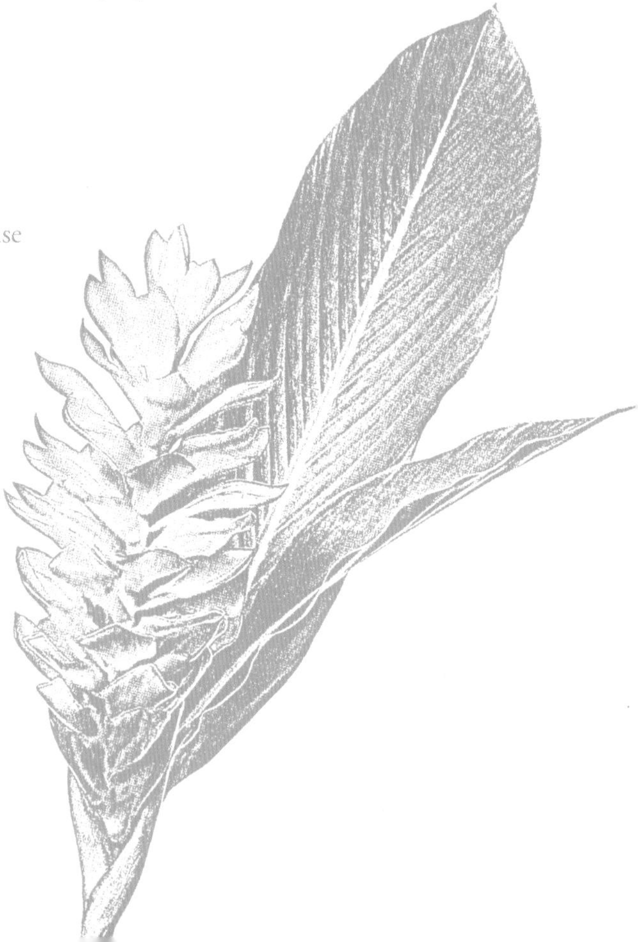

CARAMEL MIRANDA—"A SHARING DESSERT"

SERVES 4

Caramel Sauce (see recipe below)
Choose 6 to 8 of the following:

2	oz.	fresh coconut, toasted
2	oz.	Maui pineapple cubes
2	oz.	star fruit
2	oz.	raspberries
2	oz.	long-stem strawberries
2	oz.	blackberries
2	oz.	papaya
2	oz.	apple banana
2	oz.	guava
2	oz.	mango
1	oz.	white chocolate drops
1	oz.	dark chocolate drops

Macadamia nut ice cream
(2 to 4 oz. per person)

Steven Minkowski

Lace Caramel Sauce on an ovenproof plate ❧ Sprinkle with selected fruit and chocolate and heat just until hot ❧ Remove from heat ❧ Spoon ice cream in center of plate and serve immediately ❧ One plate serves four people.

CARAMEL SAUCE

11	oz. sugar	8	oz. heavy cream
5½	oz. water	1	tsp. butter
1	tsp. cream of tartar		

In a heavy saucepan over high heat whisk together sugar, water and cream of tartar, until coppery brown ❧ Remove from heat and whisk in heavy cream until cool ❧ Whisk in butter ❧ Keep at room temperature.

Chef's Suggestion: If you use dark chocolate drops, I prefer Hawaiian Vintage chocolate.

CHOCOLATE CRUNCH BARS

SERVES 6-8

1 cup diced macadamia nuts	1½ lbs. milk chocolate
¼ cup water	1¼ lbs. dark chocolate
1 cup brown sugar	2½ cups heavy whipping cream,
½ cup corn syrup	whipped to soft peaks
¼ cup butter	4 tsp. macadamia nut liqueur
½ tsp. vanilla extract	¼ cup cocoa powder for dusting
1 tsp. baking soda, sifted	Anglaise (see recipe on next page)
¼ cup macadamia nut oil or vegetable oil	Chocolate Sauce (see recipe on next page)
12 oz. gaufrette cookies (about 50)	Fresh berries for garnish

Ronario S. Collado

Mark Okumura came up with this light and crunchy chocolate dessert with an interesting, soft texture that melts in the mouth. The gaufrette cookies are the thin, crispy wafers that are typically served with ice cream.

Preheat the oven to 250°F ✽ Grease a baking sheet and spatula ✽ Line a 9" by 13" pan with plastic wrap ✽ Place the nuts on an ungreased baking sheet and toast for 10 minutes ✽ In a heavy-bottomed saucepan over medium-high heat combine water, brown sugar, corn syrup and butter ✽ Heat until the mixture reaches 280°F on a candy thermometer ✽ Add the vanilla and toasted nuts ✽ Carefully stir in the baking soda, using caution as the mixture will bubble up ✽ Immediately pour onto the greased baking sheet and spread evenly with the greased spatula ✽ When cool enough to touch, carefully pull out the brittle with your hands to make it thinner ✽ Place the brittle in a kitchen towel and crush with a rolling pin or mallet, or place in food processor and pulse into fine crumbs ✽ Transfer to a bowl and add the oil ✽ Place the gaufrette cookies in a kitchen towel and crush with a rolling pin or mallet ✽ Add to the brittle in the bowl ✽ In the top of a double boiler, melt the milk chocolate ✽ Add to the bowl ✽ Stir well and transfer the mixture to the plastic wrap–lined pan ✽ Refrigerate until needed ✽ In the top of a double boiler, melt the dark chocolate ✽ Transfer to a clean bowl ✽ When cool, fold in the heavy cream, add the liqueur, and mix thoroughly ✽ Spread over the milk chocolate mixture in the pan and refrigerate for at least 2 hours, or preferably overnight ✽ Remove the chocolate from the pan and transfer to a flat work surface ❧ Remove and discard the plastic wrap ❧ Cut the chocolate into oblong bars or desired shapes ❧ Dust with cocoa powder before serving ❧ To serve, spoon a pool of Anglaise on individual plates ❧ Swirl in the Chocolate Sauce ❧ Artistically arrange pieces of the crunch bars in a pile next to the Anglaise ❧ Garnish with the berries.

ANGLAISE

4   egg yolks
¼   cup sugar
1   cup milk

1   vanilla bean, halved
      lengthwise
      and seeds scraped

In a bowl whisk together egg yolks and sugar ❧ In a saucepan bring milk and vanilla bean and seeds to a boil ❧ Stir ½ cup of the hot milk into the egg mixture, then pour the milk and egg mixture back into the saucepan ❧ Reduce the heat to medium ❧ Cook, stirring constantly, until the mixture thickens and coats the back of a wooden spoon; do not overcook ❧ Strain into a stainless steel bowl and place in an ice bath to cool ❧ When cool, stir once more, and refrigerate until needed.

CHOCOLATE SAUCE

4   oz. dark chocolate
¼   cup heavy whipping cream
1   cup raspberries or other fresh fruit, for garnish

Place the chocolate in a small, deep bowl ❧ In a saucepan bring the heavy cream to a boil ❧ Pour over the chocolate and stir until smooth ❧ Keep at room temperature until ready to use ❧ Heat over a water bath, if the sauce becomes too thick and cold.

FIVE-SPICE CHOCOLATE MOUSSE

SERVES 4

4	oz. dark chocolate		4	Tbsp. brandy		2	egg whites, whipped
¾	oz. bitter chocolate		2	cups heavy cream		¼	cup sugar
2	egg yolks		12	gelatin leaves or 2 oz.		Chocolate Sauce (see recipe below)
5	tsp. five-spice powder			gelatin powder		

In a double boiler, melt together the dark and bitter chocolate ✹ Beat egg yolks and add to the melted chocolate ✹ Add the five-spice powder and brandy ✹ Whip heavy cream and soften gelatin ✹ Fold both into the chocolate mixture ✹ Beat egg whites and sugar until stiff ✹ Fold the egg white mixture into the melted chocolate mixture ✹ Chill ✹ When ready to serve, spoon or pipe into individual serving dishes and top with Chocolate Sauce.

CHOCOLATE SAUCE

4   oz. bitter chocolate
2   Tbsp. liquid coffee

In a saucepan, melt the chocolate in the liquid coffee; blend well.

GLENN CHU | INDIGO EURASIAN CUISINE

GOLDEN TEMPLE BANANAS

With Ginger Mint Sauce

SERVES 2

1½ oz. butter

3 oz. brown sugar

2 oz. ginger mint sauce

6 oz. banana, sliced

4 sprigs mint, julienne

Heat a sauté pan ❧ Add butter, brown sugar and ginger mint sauce ❧ Cook until sauce becomes thick ❧ Add banana and stir gently ❧ Sprinkle with mint and serve immediately.

HAWAIIAN CREAM CAKE

With Cream Cheese Frosting

MAKES 2 9-INCH LAYER CAKES (THREE LAYERS EACH)

8 oz. butter	2 tsp. baking soda	1 cup chopped macadamia nuts
8 oz. shortening	2 tsp. salt	1 cup crushed pineapple, drained
2 lbs. sugar	3 tsp. vanilla	12 egg whites
12 egg yolks	2 cups buttermilk	Cream Cheese Frosting (see recipe
1 lb. 8 oz. all-purpose flour	8 oz. shredded coconut	below)

Preheat oven to 350°F. Combine butter, shortening and sugar; cream together well. Lightly beat egg yolks and stir into butter mixture. Mix together flour, baking soda, salt and vanilla. Stir into butter mixture. Stir in buttermilk. Add coconut, macadamia nuts and crushed pineapple. Whip egg whites and fold into mixture. Butter and flour six 9" cake pans, then line with parchment. Pour batter in, distributing evenly. Tap once to settle batter. Bake until cake springs back and sides pull away from the pan and are lightly brown. Cool on racks. Spread with Cream Cheese Frosting.

CREAM CHEESE FROSTING

4 8-oz. packages cream cheese	1 tsp. vanilla extract or 1 vanilla bean scraped
Powdered sugar to taste	

Beat cream cheese in a large bowl until fluffy. Beat in powdered sugar and vanilla.

PHILIPPE PADOVANI | PADOVANI'S RESTAURANT & WINE BAR

HAWAIIAN VINTAGE CHOCOLATE MOUSSE

SERVES 4

4	oz. Hawaiian Vintage chocolate	3	Tbsp. sugar
5	egg yolks	5	egg whites

In the top of a double boiler melt the chocolate. Remove from heat and set aside. Beat egg yolks and 1 tablespoon of the sugar until very fluffy. Combine into melted chocolate. In a mixing bowl beat egg whites and progressively add the remaining 2 tablespoons of the sugar. Beat until egg whites are stiff, but not dry. Scoop about ¼ of the beaten whites onto the chocolate mixture, and using a large rubber spatula, stir them into the mixture. Gently and quickly fold in the remaining egg whites. Pour the mousse into serving dishes and refrigerate for at least 4 hours.

Franzen Photography

HAWAIIAN VINTAGE CHOCOLATE SEVEN SINS MERINGUE CAKE

SERVES 10

2	egg yolks	2	oz. Heaven and Earth Four Fruit Sauce	7½	oz. heavy cream
1	whole egg				Meringue (see recipe below)
1½	oz. sugar	5	oz. Hawaiian Vintage Chocolate		Cocoa for dusting

In a mixer at medium speed whisk egg yolks with the whole egg ❧ Cook the sugar with Heaven and Earth Four Fruit Sauce to a temperature of 260°F ❧ Pour the sugar mixture over the eggs ❧ Mix at low speed until cool ❧ Melt the chocolate ❧ Whip the cream ❧ Add a bit of the cream to the melted chocolate ❧ Incorporate the Four Fruit mixture ❧ Finish by combining all ingredients together ❧ Refrigerate mixture until set ❧ Spread a layer of mousse over a meringue layer ❧ Add another layer of meringue, then mousse ❧ Top with final meringue layer ❧ Cover entire cake with a layer of mousse ❧ Break straight meringue into 2-inch pieces, then press into cake; cover completely with meringue ❧ Dust with cocoa.

MERINGUE

⅓	cup dark cocoa powder	1	cup sugar
1½	cups powdered sugar		Parchment paper
8	oz. egg whites (8 large eggs)		

Sift cocoa and powdered sugar together ❧ Beat egg whites until stiff, then fold in cocoa and powdered sugar ❧ Draw three circles with bottom of a cake pan on parchment paper, then spray with vegetable oil ❧ Place meringue mixture into a pastry bag with a ½-inch-round tip ❧ Pipe meringue, starting from the center of each cake circle, and snail the mixture to the outlined form ❧ Repeat the process on the other two circles ❧ With the remaining meringue, pipe mixture into straight lines until all meringue is used up ❧ Bake in oven preheated to 250°F for 1 hour and 15 minutes ❧ Cool for 5 minutes then remove from paper ❧ Place meringues on cooling rack to cool completely.

DANIEL DELBREL | SHERATON MOANA SURFRIDER

LILIKO'I MOUSSE NAPOLEON

SERVES 4

Macadamia Nut Phyllo Squares (see
   recipe below)
Liliko'i Mousse (see recipe below)
Fresh fruit and fruit sauce, if desired

Place a Macadamia Nut Phyllo
Square on a dessert plate ❧ Spoon
Liliko'i Mousse in center ❧ Place
another phyllo square on top ❧
Repeat with the filling and top with
a third square ❧ Garnish with fresh
fruit and fruit sauce, if desired.

MACADAMIA NUT PHYLLO SQUARES

4	sheets phyllo dough (about 12 inches by 9 inches)	4	Tbsp. melted butter	4	Tbsp. finely chopped macadamia nuts
		6	Tbsp. granulated sugar		

Preheat oven to 375°F ❧ Handle phyllo dough according to directions on package ❧ Brush a sheet of phyllo dough with melted butter; sprinkle with sugar and finely chopped macadamia nuts ❧ Repeat steps until all four sheets are layered ❧ Cut into 4" squares ❧ Bake on a cookie sheet for approximately 5 to 6 minutes or until golden brown.

LILIKO'I MOUSSE

¼	oz. gelatin (1 envelope)	2	egg whites	1	cup heavy cream, whipped to soft peaks
7	oz. passion fruit purée	4	oz. (10 Tbsp.) sugar		

Sprinkle gelatin over passion fruit purée ❧ Warm purée and gelatin over a hot water bath until gelatin dissolves ❧ Cool to room temperature ❧ Whip egg whites to soft peaks, then add the sugar gradually ❧ Whip until stiff ❧ Fold egg whites into purée mixture, then gently fold in whipped cream.

147

MANGO BREAD

SERVES 24

8	cups flour	8	tsp. cinnamon	2	cups shredded coconut
6	cups sugar	12	eggs, lightly beaten	2	cups chopped macadamia nuts
8	tsp. baking soda	4	cups oil	2	cups golden raisins
2	tsp. salt	8	cups diced mango	4	tsp. vanilla

Preheat oven to 350°F ❧ In a bowl combine dry ingredients and mix well ❧ Add remaining ingredients and blend well ❧ Pour batter into small foil or metal loaf pans ❧ Makes about 6 or 8 loaves ❧ Bake until toothpick comes out clean ❧ Cool on racks for about 5 minutes, then remove from pans.

PALOMINO TOWER

SERVES 2

6½	oz. semisweet chocolate	3 oz. sugar
4	oz. unsalted butter	Nonstick spray
4	large eggs	Flour to coat soufflé dish

In a double boiler melt chocolate. Add the butter to the melted chocolate and blend; allow to cool to 115°F to 120°F. In a separate bowl lightly beat eggs with a whip. Add sugar to the eggs and blend well. Fold the chocolate mixture into the egg mixture and refrigerate overnight. Spray the inside of two soufflé dishes with nonstick spray. Lightly coat with flour. Fill each dish with 8-ounce weight of chocolate mixture. Bake in a convection oven at 350°F with the fan on for 10 to 12 minutes, or 400°F in a preheated oven for 15 to 18 minutes. Check for an internal temperature of 145°F. Remove from oven and allow to cool at room temperature. Refrigerate, then remove from pan. For ease of removal, gently slide a thin knife in between the cake and mold. Remove carefully. Reheat in a microwave oven for 30 seconds to warm; top with your favorite fruit sauce or whipped cream.

POHĀ BERRY BREAD PUDDING

SERVES 4

1	qt. milk	1	tsp. vanilla	½	cup pohā berry jam
1	cup sugar	1	loaf chopped French toast		Anglaise Sauce (see recipe below)
8	whole eggs		bread		
4	egg yolks				

Preheat oven to 350°F. Combine milk, sugar, whole eggs, egg yolks and vanilla; mix thoroughly, then put through a strainer. Line a 9"x13" baking pan with French toast bread and add in pohā berry jam. Cover with custard mixture to soak bread and bake in a water bath for 1½ to 2 hours. Test for doneness by poking custard with a small knife; if it comes out dry, then it's done. Cut custard into individual servings and top with Anglaise Sauce.

ANGLAISE SAUCE

1	cup milk	½	cup egg yolks	1	vanilla bean (split with seeds)
½	cup heavy cream	3	oz. sugar		or 1 tsp. vanilla extract

In a heavy saucepan heat the milk and cream. In a separate bowl mix egg yolks and sugar. When milk gets hot pour it into the egg mixture, while whisking vigorously. Add the vanilla bean. Cook to 170°F, stirring constantly with spoon. When it reaches temperature, run through a fine strainer into ice bath.

VACHERIN OF RASPBERRY SORBET

With Marinated Strawberries and Mango in Liliko'i Coulis

SERVES 4

8 Meringues (see recipe below)	Liliko'i Coulis (see recipe below)
Raspberry Sorbet (see recipe below)	4 sprigs mint
2 cups whipped cream	

Place a meringue in the center of each plate ❧ Add a scoop of raspberry sorbet on top of meringue ❧ Place another meringue on top of sorbet ❧ Decorate by piping whipped cream from a pastry bag, with a star tip, on four sides of meringue and one ring on top of the meringue ❧ Add Liliko'i Coulis ❧ Garnish with a sprig of mint on top ❧ Serve immediately.

MERINGUE

5 egg whites	1 cup confectioners' sugar
1 Tbsp. granulated sugar	½ cup granulated sugar

Preheat oven to 275°F ❧ Beat egg whites until stiff, but partway through add the 1 tablespoon sugar ❧ Sift together confectioners' sugar and ½ cup granulated sugar, then fold into egg whites ❧ (It is important not to let the meringue sit, as it tends to fall apart.) ❧ Fill a pastry bag right away and squeeze it onto a buttered and floured baking sheet or onto a baking sheet lined with parchment paper (dab a little meringue on each corner of the paper to stick it to the pan) ❧ Pipe meringue onto pan in circular shapes or to your desired shape and size ❧ Bake for 1 hour and 15 minutes (Two sheets can bake at once.) ❧ When done, the meringues should be a very light brown color and completely dry on both the top and bottom ❧ Turn oven temperature down, if meringue browns too quickly ❧ Meringue may be stored for up to 3 weeks in a metal box or a tightly closed container.

RASPBERRY SORBET

1 qt. raspberries
12 oz. granulated sugar
1 lemon, squeezed

Blend raspberries in a mixer and strain ❧ Dissolve sugar in the mixture for a few minutes ❧ Add lemon juice and mix together ❧ Place mixture in an ice cream machine and follow manufacturer's instructions.

LILIKO'I COULIS

½ cup liliko'i juice
1 cup granulated sugar
2 cups strawberries, cut into quarters
2 mangoes, sliced into wedges

Blend liliko'i juice with sugar, then strain through a fine sieve ❧ Marinate strawberries and mango in coulis and set aside.

INDEX OF RECIPES